INDO-EUROPEAN MYTH & RELIGION

A MANUAL

Second Edition

Revised Printing

Roger D. Woodard

KENDALL/HUNT PUBLISHING COMPANY
4050 Westmark Drive P.O. Box 1840 Dubuque, Iowa 52002

ISBN 13: 978-0-7575-3425-6
ISBN 10: 0-7575-3425-2

Printed in the United States of America
10 9 8 7 6 5 4

For
Stephanie
Christina
Holly
C. J.
Paul
Brooke
Matthew
Daniel

Arma virumque cano, Troiae qui primus ab oris
Italiam fato profugus Lavinaque venit
litora—multum ille et terris iactatus et alto
vi superum, saevae memorem Iunonis ob iram,
multa quoque et bello passus, dum conderet urbem
inferretque deos Latio; genus unde Latinum
Albanique patres atque altae moenia Romae.

Virgil, *Aeneid* 1.1–7

'Arms and the man I sing, who first from the coasts
Of Troy, a fugitive by fate, to Italy and Lavinian shores
Did come—much tossed on land and sea by a force
Borne from above, from raging Juno's mindful wrath,
And suffering much of war as well, until he a city should found
And carry his gods to Latium; whence the Latin race,
And lords of Alba, and the towering walls of Rome.'

Contents

Preface		**vii**
1	The Indo-Europeans	1
2	Language, Myth, and Structuralism: The Evolution of a Discipline	7
3	Roman Religion and Roman Mythic History	13
	Fasti Study Questions: Set One	35
4	The Greeks and Their Gods	37
5	Hesiod's *Theogony*	41
6	The Gods of Olympus and the Heroes of Ancient Greece	53
	Fasti Study Questions: Set Two	79
7	The Gods of Vedic India and Their Indo-European Heritage	81
	Fasti Study Questions: Set Three	99
8	The Mahabharata and Its Indo-European Heritage	101
9	The Gods of Ancient Persia and Their Indo-European Heritage	117
	Fasti Study Questions: Set Four	123
10	Celtic Society and Religion	125
	Fasti Study Questions: Set Five	147
11	Scandinavian Myth and Its Indo-European Heritage	149
	Fasti Study Questions: Set Six	171
Practice Exams		**173**
Answers to Practice Exams		**199**

Preface

The comparative study of Indo-European mythology and religion is as broad as it is intriguing. Its primary documents span the gulf of time that separates the Bronze Age of antiquity from the Middle Ages—documents authored in languages as distinct as Hittite and Old Irish, as Umbrian and Lithuanian, as Middle Iranian and Old Norse. Its primary cultures range in geographic distribution from Iceland to Central and South Asia—many diverse peoples whose heritage is anchored in a common cultural and linguistic entity called *Proto-Indo-European*. The investigation of those documents and cultures, ultimately with an eye toward recovering the religious and mythic system of the Indo-European ancestors, is a remarkably fascinating undertaking, one that uniquely combines scientific principles and methods and humanistic literary and cultural inquiry, traversing numerous disciplinary boundaries.

In the pages that follow, the reader will find a structured overview of key terms, concepts, issues, and texts for a course of study in comparative Indo-European mythology and religion. The material included is designed for coverage in a college semester of approximately fourteen weeks and so is necessarily selective. The manual can be easily tailored to shorter periods of study by further selective pruning. Conversely, the materials can be readily expanded to meet the needs of a two-semester course, or a course that focuses only on a smaller subset of the Indo-European cultures and traditions surveyed herein.

For expanding the coverage of the manual and for further investigation of particular areas, the manual user will want to refer to the works included in *Bibliography and Further Reading*, found at the end of each chapter. Using those works as a guide, expansion of coverage can be achieved with a modicum of effort. To the extent possible, only English works have been included. A few seminal works, however, are only available in a language other than English—most notably, works in French by Georges Dumézil, the leading figure in the comparative study of Indo-European myth and religion throughout most of the twentieth century. An especially useful book written in English that summarizes the development of much of Dumézil's thought and work and responses thereto by both supporters and critics is C. Scott Littleton's *The New Comparative Mythology* (University of California Press). A second work that will prove to be of great value to the non-French reader is Jaan Puhvel's *Comparative Mythology* (Johns Hopkins University Press). Puhvel summarizes on a culture-by-culture basis many of the mythic and religious traditions of several Indo-European cultures and Dumézilian interpretations of those traditions. He follows the survey of Indo-European cultures with discussions of recurring Indo-European mythic themes.

The *Manual* includes sample examinations, each set of which covers approximately one-third of the material that might be presented in a semester-long course. Answers to the examination questions can be found at the back of the book, following the sample examinations. The student user of this book will find the sample examinations a helpful exercise for both learning and evaluating the success of the learning process; early and frequent practice with the examinations is encouraged. Instructors are free to utilize and adapt the sample exams as desired.

Also included in the *Manual* are exercises linked to the Penguin edition of Ovid's *Fasti* (Boyle and Woodard, 2004). Among primary documents, Ovid's *Fasti* is a singularly rich source of information for the study of ancient Roman religion—a religious (and mythic) tradition especially valuable for the recovery of the primitive Indo-European traditions. The questions that appear in *Fasti Study Questions* are drawn both from the text of the poem and, especially, from the extensive notes included in the Penguin edition of Boyle and Woodard. Those notes comprise a detailed commentary on Roman religion, Greek myth, and Indo-European myth and religion that complements and supplements the contents of the *Manual*. Qualified instructors can receive answers to the *Fasti Study Questions* by sending a request on departmental letterhead to the author of the present work (Roger D. Woodard, MFAC 338, Department of Classics, University of Buffalo, Buffalo, NY 14261).

The author wishes to express his appreciation to Michael Funke and the helpful editorial staff at Kendall/Hunt Publishing. Appreciation and thanks are again due to Paul and Katherine for their unflagging and loving support and toleration during the preparation of another manuscript. I dedicate this book to *les cousins*, especially Christina, who, unawares, implanted in my mind the idea for this project.

Postscript for instructors: When I first began to develop a course in Indo-European myth and religion—a few years ago now, at Johns Hopkins (a place with a rich heritage in the study of ancient Indo-European cultures and languages)—I cast about for a pedagogical model that I could use to disseminate efficiently and manageably to students the large and diverse body of material that such a study entails. What I hooked was Georges Dumézil, and what I then discovered was that Dumézil's model of primitive Indo-European society and Indo-European myth and epic makes for a remarkably effective pedagogical tool—a means of drawing together what might at first appear to be a disparate collection of far-flung traditions. In the years since, I have had the good fortune of teaching these materials to many thousands of students. On the basis of that experience, I would urge instructors to allot sufficient class time through the course of the teaching term to tell the ancient tales. It is a remarkable experience; I think of it as the practice of a kind of "cognitive archaeology." The ancient stories are no less captivating now than when they were told millennia ago. As we listen to those tales and experience the emotions bound up in them, much as people of ages long past listened to those tales and experienced the emotions bound up in them, we come face to face with ancient humankind in a way that eclipses most other efforts to bridge the chasm of time, and our differences, past and present, seem diminished.

1 The Indo-Europeans

Outline of Key Terms and Concepts

1. The Proto-Indo-European Community and Homeland

    The primitive Indo-European community likely existed as a socio-cultural entity between the fifth and third millennia BC.

    Differentiation into descendent cultures had already begun in the latter portion of this period.

    The most likely location of the Proto-Indo-European homeland is perhaps the Pontic Steppe.

    There is little consensus in this matter.

    Scholars have proposed many locales across Europe and Asia.

    An early Indo-European community (though not the Proto-Indo-European community) is very probably to be identified with the Kurgan Culture of the south of the Ukraine and Russia (Gimbutas).

    From the homeland, Indo-European peoples dispersed and moved across Europe and into Asia.

    Indo-European languages completely displaced the "Old European" languages (i.e., those spoken in Europe before the arrival of the Indo-Europeans).

    Basque is perhaps the single exception.

    With Indo-European expansion in Eurasia, the parent language of Proto-Indo-European evolves into a family of languages.

2. The Indo-European language family consists of ten major subfamilies, most of which have further large subdivisions.

    The following survey is not exhaustive; for a fuller listing consult *The American Heritage Dictionary of Indo-European Roots*, pp. 148–149 (following the practice of the dictionary, extinct languages are here shown in italics):

    Germanic

    West Germanic: English, Frisian, Dutch, German

    East Germanic: *Gothic*

    North Germanic: Norwegian, Swedish, Danish, Icelandic, Faeroese

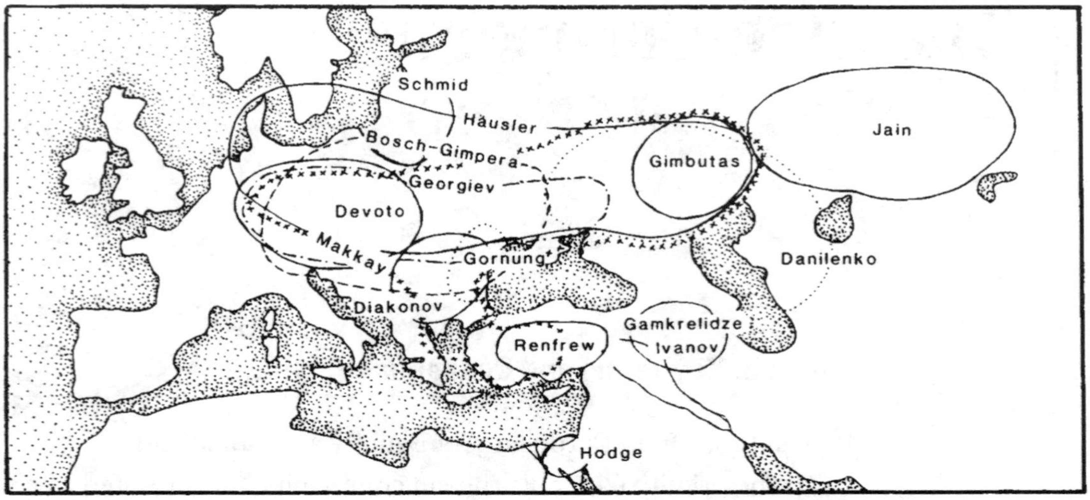

Map 1–1 Some proposed locations of the Indo-European homeland.

Celtic

- p-Celtic or Brythonic: Welsh, Breton, *Cornish*
- q-Celtic of Goidelic: Irish, Scots Gaelic, Manx

Italic

- Sabellian: *Oscan, Umbrian, Paelignian, Marrucinian, Volscian, Sabine*
- Latino-Faliscan: *Faliscan, Latin*
  - From Latin the modern Romance languages evolved: Portuguese, Spanish, Catalan, Provençal, French, Italian, Rhaeto-Romance, Romanian

Hellenic

- Ancient Greek dialects: *Mycenaean Greek, Attic-Ionic, Aeolic, Doric, Northwest Greek, Arcado-Cypriot*
- Modern Greek

Anatolian

- Second millennium BC: *Hittite, Palaic, Luvian*
- First millennium BC: *Lydian, Lycian*

Balto-Slavic

- Baltic: Lithuanian, Latvian, *Old Prussian*
- Slavic
  - South Slavic: *Old Church Slavic*, Bulgarian, Macedonian, Serbo-Croatian, Slovenian
  - West Slavic: Polish, Sorbian, Czech, Slovak
  - East Slavic: Russian, Byelorussian, Ukrainian

Indo-Iranian

- Indic: *Sanskrit, Pali*, Hindi, Sindhi, Punjabi, Urdu, Gujurati
- Iranian: *Avestan, Old Persian*, Farsi, Kurdish, Pashto

Armenian

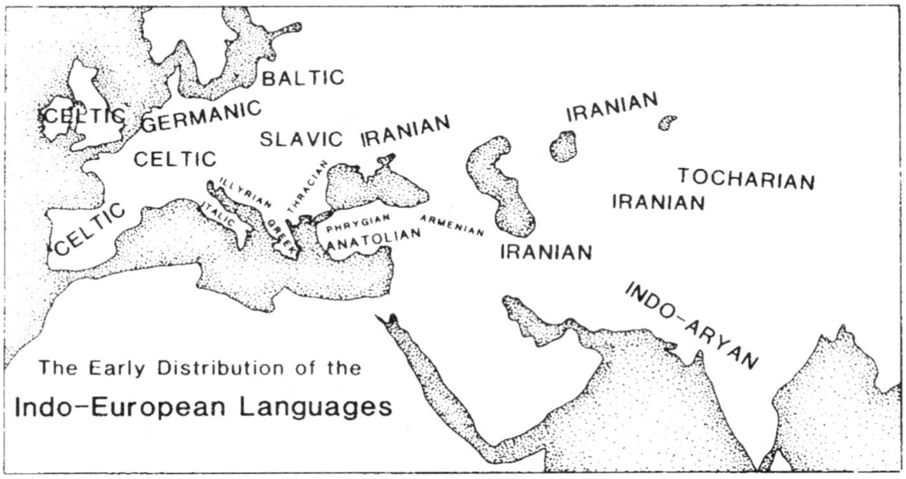

Map 1–2 The early distribution of the Indo-European languages.

Albanian

Gheg

Tosk

Tocharian

Tocharian A

Tocharian B

In addition to the ten major subfamilies, there are several so-called "minor Indo-European languages" (less well attested), such as Phrygian, Thracian, and Illyrian.

Centum and Satem languages

The terms *Centum* and *Satem* denote two major sets of Indo-European subfamilies.

Set membership is determined by the developmental treatment of the Proto-Indo-European palatal, velar, and labiovelar consonants.

Centum languages are generally the more western subfamilies.

Centum is the Latin word for 'hundred'.

Italic, Celtic, Germanic, Hellenic, Anatolian, Tocharian

Tocharian is the exception to the geographic generalization.

Tocharian was spoken in present-day western China.

Satem languages are generally the more eastern subfamilies.

Satem is from *satəm*, the Avestan word for 'hundred'.

Indo-Iranian, Balto-Slavic, Armenian, Albanian

3. The comparative method of historical linguistics

The linguistic method used to reconstruct prehistoric parent languages by comparing historically attested daughter languages is called the *comparative method of historical linguistics.*

The method is possible only because sound change is regular.

The Great Vowel Shift of English provides an example of the regularity of sound change.

About 1500 AD the accented long vowels of English changed.

Among other changes:

- The high front vowel /ī/ became the diphthong /aI/ /mīs/ became /maIs/ 'mice'
- The high back vowel /ū/ became the diphthong /aU/ /mūs/ became /maUs/ 'mouse'
- The mid-front vowel /ē/ became the high front vowel /ī/ /gēs/ became /gīs/ 'geese'
- The mid-back vowel /ō/ became the high back vowel /ū/ /gōs/ became /gūs/ 'goose'

Cognates

Cognates may be defined as "related words in sister languages that develop from a common form in the parent language."

For example, Greek *lānos*, Latin *lāna*, Welsh *gwlan*, Sanskrit *ūrṇā*, Lithuanian *vìlna*, and Gothic *wulla* are Indo-European cognates meaning 'wool,' all having descended from the same Proto-Indo-European word-root.

Cognates can then, conversely, be used to reconstruct an ancestral word-form as it existed in the parent language.

On the basis of the above (and additional) cognates, the Proto-Indo-European root for 'wool' can be reconstructed as *$welh_2$-.

The above cognates are descended from a form of that root to which an *n*-suffix has been attached.

Bibliography and Further Reading

Fortson, Benjamin. 2004. *Indo-European Language and Culture: An Introduction.* Oxford: Blackwell.

Fox, Anthony. 1995. *Linguistic Reconstruction: An Introduction to Theory and Method.* Oxford: Oxford University Press.

Gimbutas, Maria. 1985. "Primary and Secondary Homeland of the Indo-Europeans." *Journal of Indo-European Studies* 13: 185–202.

Hoenigswald, Henry, Roger Woodard, and James P. T. Clackson. 2004. "Indo-European." In Woodard 2004, pp. 534–550.

Mallory, J. P. 1989. *In Search of the Indo-Europeans.* London: Thames and Hudson.

Mallory, J. P., and D. Q. Adams. 1997. *Encyclopedia of Indo-European Culture.* London and Chicago: Fitzroy Dearborn Publishers.

Ringe, Donald. 2004. "Reconstructed Ancient Languages." In Woodard 2004, pp. 1112–1128.

Watkins, Calvert. 2000. *The American Heritage Dictionary of Indo-European Roots*. 2nd ed. Boston: Houghton Mifflin.

Woodard, Roger. 2004. *The Cambridge Encyclopedia of the World's Ancient Languages*. Cambridge: Cambridge University Press.

2 Language, Myth, and Structuralism: The Evolution of a Discipline

Outline of Key Terms and Concepts

1. Structuralism

    The scholarly study of myth during the twentieth century was closely linked to the interpretative method called *structuralism.*

    The term *structuralism* is broad in scope, owing to the diffusion of the method into many disciplines.

    For the sake of having a working definition, one may define structuralism as follows:

        Structuralism is a method of analysis in which the central tenet is that the significance of individual parts of a structure is determined by their position within the structure.

2. Ferdinand de Saussure (1857–1913)

    Ferdinand de Saussure was a professor of linguistics at the University of Geneva in the early twentieth century.

    Saussure had been trained as an historical linguist, and among his early work was an influential analysis of vowel alternation in Proto-Indo-European.

    At Geneva, Saussure developed a course in synchronic (or general) linguistics.

        Synchronic linguistics is the study of language as it exists at some moment in time.

        As opposed to synchronic linguistics, diachronic linguistics is the study of language as it changes over time.

    Saussure's synchronic analysis of language focuses on linguistic structures and the significance of individual elements within structured systems.

        For example, a consonant or vowel sound of a given language only acquires linguistic significance by its distinctness from other members of the set of sounds used by that language.

    Following Saussure's death, some of his students collaborated to write *A Course in General Linguistics* (1916), drawing from their collective class notes.

    Saussure is considered to be the founder of the modern study of general linguistics, and *A Course in General Linguistics* is regarded as the founding document.

3. Russian Formalism

   Among de Saussure's students was a young Russian, Sergei Karcevski.

   In 1917, Karcevski returned to Russia, taking with him Saussure's ideas about the structural analysis of language.

   In Russia, Saussure's theories gave rise to a school of structural analysis called *Russian Formalism.*

   Russian Formalism developed two intellectual centers:

      The Moscow Linguistic Circle was concerned chiefly with language analysis.

      The Petrograd Society for the Study of Poetic Language was concerned chiefly with a "morphological approach" to literary analysis.

   Vladimir Propp

      Vladimir Propp was a product of The Petrograd Society for the Study of Poetic Language.

      Propp authored *The Morphology of the Folk Tale* (1928).

         Propp argues that all folk tales (fairy tales) have a common universal structure.

         Propp defines that structure as a sequence of functions: F1, F2, F3, . . . F31.

         Propp defines a *function* as "an action performed by some character."

            Functions are persistent (though particular functions may be optionally deleted), but the character performing the action of the function varies from tale to tale.

   Saussurian structuralism spread across Europe in the following decades.

      Two Russian-born linguists, Nikolay Trubetskoy (1890–1938) and Roman Jakobson (1896–1982) became central figures in the development of the structural school of linguistic analysis called *Prague School Structuralism.*

4. Claude Lévi-Strauss (b. 1908)

   In the mid-twentieth century, Claude Lévi-Strauss, a French anthropologist, applied linguistic structuralist methods to the analysis of anthropological problems.

      Lévi-Strauss was particularly influenced by the work of Trubetskoy and Jakobson.

   Lévi-Strauss argued that myth is itself a kind of language; like language, myth consists of structural units.

   Lévi-Strauss's ideas about the structural analysis of myth are presented in his article "The Structural Study of Myth" (1955).

   The structural unit of myth is the *mytheme:* "a bundle of relations."

MYTHEMES

1	2	3	4
Cadmus looks for Europa, his sister.		Cadmus slays the dragon.	
	Spartoi slay one another.		
	Oedipus kills Laius, his father.		Laius ("left-sided")
			Son of Labdacus ("lame")
		Oedipus slays The Sphinx.	
Oedipus weds Jocasta, his mother.			Oedipus ("swollen-foot")
	Eteocles kills Polynices, his brother.		
Antigone buries Polynices, her brother, though the king forbids it.			

Figure 2–1 The Oedipus Myth (adapted from Claude Lévi-Strauss, 1955).

Relation is not explicitly defined, but is illustrated.

Lévi-Strauss patterned his mythic structural unit, the mytheme, after the linguistic unit called the *phoneme*.

A phoneme is a unit of sound structure (consonant or vowel).

At the time of Lévi-Strauss's article, structural linguists, such as Jakobson, were analyzing the phoneme as consisting of "a bundle of distinctive features."

Distinctive features are binary properties of sounds, such as ± lip-rounding, ± tongue height, ± vocal cord vibration, and so forth.

Lévi-Strauss illustrates his structural analysis with the Oedipus myth: See Figure 2–1.

Each column represents a mytheme.

Each item in a column is a relation.

Mytheme 1: The overrating of blood relations.

There is too much intimacy associated with each relation.

Mytheme 2: The underrating of blood relations.

There is too little intimacy associated with each relation.

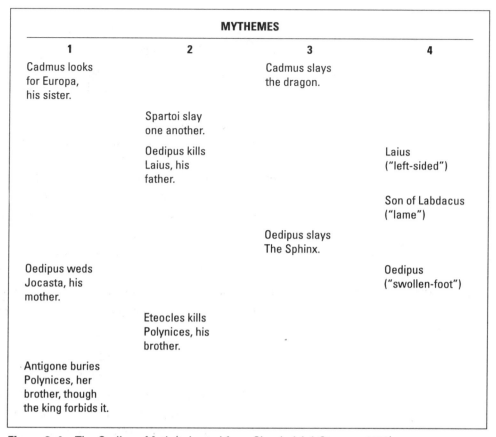

Mytheme 3: The denial of autochthonous origin.

Autochthonous refers to the common notion that humans have their origin from the earth.

In this instance, armed men, the Spartoi, sprang up when Cadmus planted the dragon's teeth in the earth.

The relations in this column involve the slaying of that dragon and another monster (a duplicate of the first relation)—a human denial of autochthonous origin, in the view of Lévi-Strauss.

Mytheme 4: The affirmation of authochthonous origin.

In traditions of the autochthonous origin of humans, those who come out of the ground often display some disability.

The relations in this column are associated with disability (including left-handedness)—an affirmation of autochthonous origin.

Column 1 is to column 2 as column 4 is to column 3.

Columns 1 and 2 concern the realm of human experience.

Human life produces human life (family).

Columns 3 and 4 concern the realm of belief.

The earth produces human life.

Human experience contradicts theory or belief.

But even within the realm of experience, there is contradiction (the + and − relationship of columns 1 and 2).

This observation allows us to live with the contradictions between experience and belief.

The Oedipus myth provides a means of coming to grips with such contradiction, as revealed by structural analysis, claims Lévi-Strauss.

Lévi-Strauss's work in structural anthropology exerted great influence on other academic disciplines, such as comparative literature and philosophy, in France and beyond.

5. Georges Dumézil (1898–1986)

Dumézil was a French scholar, trained in the French school of Indo-European linguistics.

Dumézil was the leading figure in the study of comparative Indo-European myth and religion during the twentieth century.

Dumézil interpreted the fundamental characteristic of prehistoric Indo-European society to be its tripartite structure.

Dumézil used the term *function* (not to be confused with Propp's *functions*) for the structural elements of primitive Indo-European culture and society.

- First function: the realm of sovereignty

  A priestly class embodies this function.

- Second function: the realm of physical dominance and force

  A class of warriors embodies this function.

- Third function: the realm of fertility

  A class of agriculturalists, herdsmen, shepherds, and other goods producers embodies this function.

Some of the best evidence for this structure (tripartition) survives in the myths and religions of the descendent Indo-European cultures.

Though his interpretation of Indo-European culture is fundamentally structural in nature, Dumézil did not consider himself to be a "structuralist" in the sense in which the term was used in French academics of the mid-twentieth century.

Bibliography and Further Reading

De George, Richard, and Fernande De George. 1972. *The Structuralists.* Garden City, N.Y.: Doubleday.

Hawkes, Terence. 1977. *Structuralism and Semiotics.* Berkeley and Los Angeles: University of California Press.

Lévi-Strauss, Claude. "The Structural Study of Myth." *Journal of American Folklore* 78 (1955): 428–444.

Littleton, Scott. 1982. *The New Comparative Mythology.* 3rd ed. Berkeley and Los Angeles: University of California Press.

Propp, Vladimir. 1984. *Morphology of the Folktale.* Translated by Laurence Scott. Austin: University of Texas Press.

Puhvel, Jaan. 1987. *Comparative Mythology.* Baltimore: Johns Hopkins University Press.

Saussure, Ferdinand de. 1988. *A Course in General Linguistics.* Translated by Roy Harris. La Salle, Ill.: Open Court.

Wittig, Susan. 1975. *Structuralism: An Interdisciplinary Study.* Pittsburgh: Pickwick Press.

3 Roman Religion and Roman Mythic History

Outline of Key Terms and Concepts

1. The Flamens and their gods (Dumézil 1996)

   The *Flamines* are fifteen ancient priests of Rome.

   Each flamen is dedicated to a separate deity.

   There are twelve Minor Flamens (*Flamines Minores*).

   There are three Major Flamens (*Flamines Maiores*).

   - The Flamen Dialis: Priest of Jupiter
   - The Flamen Martialis: Priest of Mars
   - The Flamen Quirinalis: Priest of Quirinus

   Georges Dumézil proposed in his 1935 work *Flamen-Brahman* that "Flamen" and "Brahman," the names of ancient priests of Rome and India respectively, are cognates.

   The Proto-Indo-European ancestral term could be reconstructed as $*b^hlag^hs$-*men*.

   Other scholars, such as Émile Benveniste (1969), judged Dumézil's reconstruction to be problematic.

   For example, a Pre-Latin form **flags-men-* would have to be posited, for which there is no good evidence.

   Vedic *Brahman* does, however, find a cognate in Old Persian *brazman*, a term denoting appropriateness for ritual use.

   Dumézil subsequently modified his proposal (see Dumézil 1988).

   Even if the terms are not strictly cognate, many common and unusual constraints govern the day-to-day behavior of the Roman Flamen Dialis and the Indic Brahmin (Dumézil 1935; 1988).

   The Flamen Dialis cannot be forced to swear an oath.

   The Brahmin cannot be called as a witness.

   The Flamen Dialis must not look upon the army.

   The Brahmin must not conduct religious operations in the vicinity of combat.

   The Flamen Dialis must neither ride a horse nor touch a horse (even a sacrificial horse).

   The Brahmin must not study sacred texts on horseback.

The Flamen Dialis must not come near a funeral pyre.

The Brahmin must not come in contact with smoke from a funeral pyre and must desist from his studies in a village where a funeral procession is being held.

The Flamen Dialis must not touch bread fermented with yeast and cannot become intoxicated.

The Brahmin must not drink alcoholic beverage.

The Flamen Dialis must not anoint himself with oil in the open air.

The Brahmin can anoint his head with oil, but the oil must not touch any other part of his body.

The Flamen Dialis must not touch uncooked meat.

The Brahmin must only eat meat that has been offered as a sacrifice, and he cannot accept anything from the owner of a slaughterhouse.

The Flamen Dialis must not touch a dog, and he must not say the word for 'dog' (*canis*).

The Brahmin must not read the Vedas while he can hear a dog barking, and he must not eat food that has been in contact with a dog.

The Flamen Dialis must never remove his priestly cap (this was so originally, but was later changed); his wife, the Flaminica Dialis, must not ascend above the third step of a stairway, except one that is enclosed (so as to prevent others from seeing beneath her robe).

The Brahmin must never disrobe fully and he must never see his wife, the Brahmani, fully unclothed.

The shared set of highly idiosyncratic constraints in Rome and India suggests a common origin in an early period of Indo-European cultural unity.

The Flamen Dialis: Priest of Jupiter, the sky-god and king of gods (Dumézil 1996)

Still other constraints are imposed upon the Flamen Dialis.

Some constraints are intended to keep the Flamen Dialis in constant contact with the earth of Rome.

The bed of the Flamen Dialis is covered with a thin coat of clay.

The Flamen Dialis must not be absent from the bed for three successive nights.

Other constraints reflect the character of Jupiter, the sky-god, whom the Flamen and Flaminica Dialis serve.

Eventually the Flamen Dialis is permitted to remove his priestly cap indoors, but even then he must not remove it in the open air.

The Flamen Dialis must not remove his inner tunic beneath the open sky (under the eye of Jupiter).

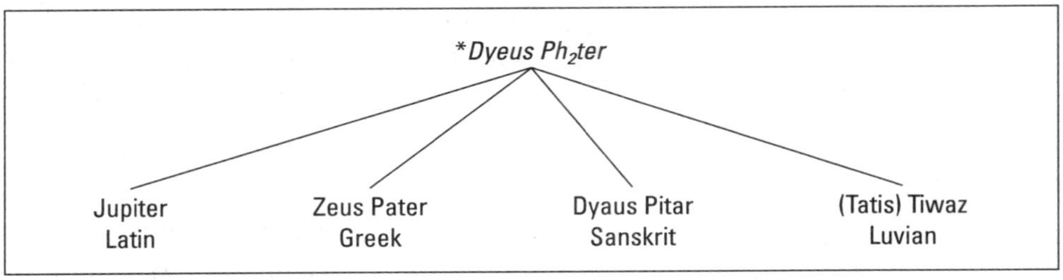

Figure 3–1 Cognate names of the Sky-God.

If the Flaminica Dialis should hear a thunderclap, she must refrain from performing her duties until she has appeased the gods.

The Latin divine name (theonym) *Jupiter*, that is *Jove Pater* ('Jove the Father'), is from earlier **Diove Pater*.

The Latin name is descended from Proto-Indo-European **Dyeus* Ph_2ter; the name of the sky-god of the primitive Indo-Europeans.

**Dyeus* is from the root **deiw-*, 'to shine'; see Figure 3–1.

**Dyeus* Ph_2ter ('Dyeus the Father')

In Rome, Jupiter remains the celestial sky-god, but he is also the sovereign god.

Jupiter's role as sovereign deity is reflected by certain legal and political aspects of the office of the Flamen Dialis.

The Flamen Dialis is closely affiliated with the *rex* ('king').

The Flamen Dialis is permitted to sit in a curule chair.

A curule chair (*sella curulis*) is a stool-like chair with curved legs, on which only the highest-ranking dignitaries are permitted to sit.

The Flamen Dialis is permitted to sit in the senate.

The Flamen Dialis frees any prisoner who is able to escape and make his way to the Flamen's house (the *Flaminia*).

The Flamen Martialis: Priest of Mars

Far less is known about the Flamen Martialis than the Flamen Dialis.

The Flamen Martialis is permitted to touch a horse.

Mars is the god of war and the horse the preeminent war-animal.

The Flamen Martialis is very likely the officiating priest at the Equus October ('October Horse').

The Equus October is a sacrifice celebrated annually on the Ides of October (October 15).

At this festival, a horse is sacrificed to Mars on the Campus Martius (the practice ground of the army).

The Flamen Quirinalis: Priest of Quirinus

The god Quirinus is a shadowy figure; to understand him, Dumézil examines the rituals in which his priest plays a role.

- The Summer Consualia; August 21 (Tertullian, *Spect.* 5)
  - The Summer Consualia are celebrated for Consus, god of stored grain.
  - The festival is held in the Circus Maximus.
    - The Circus Maximus was the major chariot race course in Rome, located between the Palatine and Aventine hills.
  - The Vestal Virgins assist the Flamen Quirinalis as he officiates at the Summer Consualia.
  - Consus is worshipped at a subterranean altar, buried beneath the turning post of the racecourse.
    - Each year the altar is excavated for the festival and then reburied.
- The Robigalia: April 25 (Ovid, *Fasti* 4.901–942)
  - The Robigalia are celebrated for Robigo/Robigus: deity of wheat rust.
  - The ritual is conducted outside of Rome in a grove on the fifth milestone of the road called the Via Claudia.
  - The sacrifice of a dog and sheep is offered to the deity.
  - Ovid records the prayer of the Flamen Quirinalis to the deity on behalf of the new grain crop.
- The Quirinalia: February 17
  - The Quirinalia are celebrated for Quirinus.
    - No ancient sources specify who the officiating priest is, but the presence of the Flamen of Quirinus is quite probable.
  - The only known rite performed on the day of the Quirinalia is the *Stultorum feriae*, 'feast of fools'.
    - Ancient Rome is divided into thirty population units called *curiae*.
    - Each *curia* is to choose a date between February 5 and 17 on which it will observe the Fornacalia, festival of Fornax.
      - Fornax is goddess of the ovens.
      - The Fornacalia are the festival of the roasting of grain.
        - If people should miss the observance of the Fornacalia designated by their *curiae*, they can make up the celebration at the *Stultorum feriae*.
- The Larentalia: December 23
  - The Larentalia are the celebration of Acca Larentia.

There are two figures identified by the name Acca Larentia in Roman tradition:

- The foster mother of Romulus, founder of Rome, and his twin brother Remus.
- A prostitute who became extremely wealthy by marriage and willed all of her belongings to the Roman people.

Little is known about the Larentalia.

Both the Flamen Quirinalis and the priests called the Pontifices (see below) play a role.

The festival is celebrated in the Velabrum, an area between the Capitoline and Palatine Hills.

On the basis of the first three festivals, Dumézil concludes:

Quirinus is the Roman god of grain.

Through his priest, Quirinus is affiliated with three grain festivals:

- The Robigalia: concerned with the young grain crop
- The Consualia: concerned with the storage of grain
- The Quirinalia: concerned with roasting of grain

Quirinus is a collaborative deity.

The priest of Quirinus takes part in observances dedicated to other deities (Consus, Robigo, Fornax).

The name of Quirinus developed from Pre-Latin **Co-virio-* 'assemblage of people'.

The Quirinalia is linked to the full set of the Roman *curiae* through the collective, final celebration of the Fornacalia.

The Pre-Capitoline Triad

The three gods served by the Major Flamens are the three chief deities of archaic Rome:

- Jupiter: the sky god and sovereign god
- Mars: the god of war
- Quirinus: the god of grain

These gods then represent the realms of the three primitive Indo-European functions.

The Romans have preserved a much earlier Indo-European tripartition as a religious structure and ideology:

- Jupiter: first function (sovereignty)
- Mars: second function (war)
- Quirinus: third function (agricultural and goods production)

The poorly documented Larentalia, December festival of Acca Larentia, lies within the sphere of the third function as well (even if there is no affiliation with grain).

Acca Larentia, the shepherdess, is clearly affiliated with third-function activities of animal care.

Acca Larentia, the wealthy prostitute, is no less a third-function figure.

The third function is also the realm of wealth and sensuality.

Plutarch (first/second centuries AD), writing in Greek, states that the "priest of Ares" (Mars?) takes part in the Larentalia (*Life of Romulus* 4.3; Plutarch says the festival is celebrated in April).

The Latin author Macrobius (fourth/fifth centuries AD) writes that the Larentalia are a festival of Jupiter (*Saturnalia* 1.10.11).

If Plutarch and Macrobius are not in error, the Larentalia would be yet another festival in which the Flamen of Quirinus cooperates with other deities and their priests, and one in which all three members of the Pre-Capitoline triad have a part.

2. Janus: God of entrances and beginnings

Janus is biform (facing in two directions).

Janus' name is from Latin *ianus* 'archway'.

Many Indo-European cognates exist: for example, Sanskrit *yānam* 'way'; Old Irish *ath* 'ford'.

Dumézil analyzes Janus as one of the "first gods" (*dieux premiers*).

These are the first gods to be invoked in a ritual.

The affiliation of these Indo-European gods spans the three functions of society; they are trifunctional.

Dumézil analyzes others as "last gods" (*dieux derniers*).

These are the last gods to be invoked in a ritual.

These gods are also trifunctional.

An example of a last god is provided by Agni.

Agni is the Indic god of fire.

Agni may also function as a first god.

A last god in Rome is Vesta.

Vesta is the Roman goddess of the hearth.

Greek Hestia, goddess of the hearth, may share a common origin and a cognate name with Vesta.

Hestia, however, is a first god.

3. Vesta

Vesta has a circular "temple" in the Roman Forum.

The structure is not technically a "temple," which by definition must be rectangular.

Within Vesta's temple burns the sacred flame of Rome.

The Vestal Virgins: Priestesses who serve Vesta

The Vestals are chosen from prominent families and begin their service to the goddess between six and ten years of age.

The Vestals serve for thirty years.

The chief duty of the Vestals is to tend the sacred flame of Rome burning within Vesta's temple.

Any water required by the Vestals is carefully controlled.

Each day's supply of water is brought in a *futile*, a vessel with a small base and a wide mouth that must be held to prevent it from tipping over.

The Vestals are chosen and supervised by the priest called the Pontifex Maximus.

If the sacred flame should go out, the Pontifex Maximus scourges the Vestals, and they then must kindle a new flame by friction.

For generating the new flame, wood from an *arbor felix* ('auspicious tree') must be utilized.

A flame so produced is seen as rooted in the earth and assures that Rome's security is rooted in the earth (Dumézil 1996).

The Vestals also prepare sacred brine and sacred flour.

These are mixed and sprinkled on Rome's sacrificial animals.

The Vestals must preserve their virginity.

Dumézil (1996) notes the ambiguous status of virginity in "primitive societies."

It is intermediate between masculinity and femininity.

This is reflected in Rome by the Vestal's enjoyment of certain legal rights normally reserved for men.

If a Vestal should lose her virginity, she is entombed alive in a subterranean chamber called the *campus sceleratus*.

The Vestal's partner is executed.

4. Protecting deities

The Penates: spirits (*numina*) of the cupboard (*penus*)

The Penates are associated with Vesta.

The Penates are worshipped at the household hearth at mealtime.

Aeneas, a Trojan, is said to have brought the Penates to Italy from Troy.

The Penates protect both the Roman household and the Roman state (*Penates publici*).

The Lares: spirits also associated with the Roman household and state.

The Lares are possibly of rural origin.

Like the Penates, the Lares are worshipped at the household hearth.

The *Lar familiaris* protects the entire household (including slaves).

The *Lares compitales* are Lares of the crossroads.

They are worshipped at crossroads, where a tower and altars are set up for them.

A festival, the Compitalia, is held in their honor in late December or early January.

Crossroads are typically places of adjoining boundaries; each bounded space has its own protecting Lares.

There is thus an assemblage of Lares at crossroads.

Among the Irish Celts, boundaries are seen to be seams in the earth, through which spirits can pass.

The *Lares praestites* are the Lares that protect Rome.

The *Lares permarini* are Lares that protect mariners.

Lares are broadly associated with all spaces of human activity.

5. The Capitoline triad: Jupiter, Juno, Minerva

In the sixth century BC, the archaic Pre-Capitoline triad (Jupiter, Mars, Quirinus) was replaced by a new (partially overlapping) triad of chief deities.

The Capitoline triad, consisting of one god and two goddesses, does not look to be typically Indo-European.

Is the Capitoline triad of Greek origin?

Each member of the triad is matched by a Greek deity:

- Jupiter = Zeus
- Juno = Hera
- Minerva = Athena

The Greeks are also an Indo-European people, but were themselves greatly influenced by non-Indo-European peoples.

The Greek travel-author Pausanias (second century AD) writes of these three Greek gods (Zeus, Hera, and Athena) being worshipped together in a temple in Phocis.

A direct link between the triad of Phocis and the much earlier Capitoline triad is not likely.

Is the Capitoline triad of Etruscan origin?

The Etruscans are a non-Indo-European people of Italy who would exert cultural influence on the Romans.

The origin of the Etruscans is uncertain and was a matter of disagreement even in antiquity.

The Greek historian Herodotus (fifth century BC), for example, claims the Etruscans came from Lydia in Asia Minor.

The Roman antiquarian Varro (second century BC) and the Greek historian of Rome, Dionysius of

Halicarnassus (first century BC) deny the claim that Lydia is the Etruscan homeland.

Evidence for Etruscans in Italy appears in the archaeological record in about the eighth century BC.

The Tarquin kings, who have an Etruscan affiliation, rule Rome from about 616 BC to 509 BC.

The Tarquins build the temple of Jupiter Optimus Maximus, in which the Capitoline triad is housed.

The Etruscan language is relatively well attested, but less well understood.

The language shows clear affinities to two meagerly attested languages:

Lemnian, from the Aegean island of Lemnos (sixth century BC), lying close to Asia Minor (where Lydia is located)

Rhaetic, from the Alps (as early as the fifth century BC)

The Etruscan alphabet is based on the Greek alphabet.

The Etruscans probably learned to write from Greeks living in the south of Italy in the eighth century BC.

The Etruscan alphabet is the source of the Latin alphabet of the Romans.

The Etruscans were themselves influenced by Greek mythic traditions.

6. Founding figures in Roman tradition (Livy 1.1–6.3; Plutarch, *Life of Romulus* 2.1–9.3)

Aeneas

Aeneas is a Trojan warrior who fled from the city of Troy when it fell to the Greeks, accompanied by his father, his son, and other Trojans.

Aeneas is the son of Anchises, a mortal, and the Greek goddess Aphrodite.

Aeneas is father of Ascanius.

Ascanius' mother perished at Troy.

After many travels and adventures, Aeneas and his Trojans come to Italy.

There Aeneas meets Lavinia, daughter of Latinus, ruler of Latium.

Aeneas wishes to marry Lavinia.

According to the Latin poet Virgil (first century BC), Lavinia is engaged to Turnus, an Italian warrior and king of the Rutuli.

Aeneas and his Trojans, with their Etruscan allies, go to war against the armies of Turnus.

Aeneas slays Turnus and marries Lavinia.

Aeneas founds the city of Lavinium.

After the death of Aeneas, his son Ascanius leaves Lavinium and founds the city of Alba Longa.

Numitor

In the lineage of the Aenean kings of Alba Longa stands Numitor.

Amulius, Numitor's brother, usurps the throne.

Amulius kills the sons of Numitor and causes Numitor's daughter, Rhea Silvia, to become a Vestal Virgin, so as to prevent her from producing an heir to the throne.

Mars, the god of war, impregnates the Vestal Rhea Silvia.

Rhea Silvia gives birth to twin sons, Romulus and Remus.

Romulus and Remus

After the birth of the twins, Amulius kills or imprisons Rhea Silvia.

Amulius sets Romulus and Remus adrift in the Tiber River.

The twins wash ashore near the Palatine Hill.

A she-wolf nurses Romulus and Remus, and a woodpecker (the bird sacred to Mars) brings them food.

A herdsman, Faustulus, finds the twins; he and his wife, Acca Larentia, bring them up.

Romulus and Remus grow up as shepherds.

Romulus and Remus are reunited with Numitor, their grandfather, after Remus becomes embroiled in a conflict with shepherds of Alba Longa and is interrogated by Numitor.

Numitor joins forces with Romulus and Remus and together with their followers they overthrow Amulius, whom Romulus kills.

Romulus and Remus decide to found a city of their own, the city of Rome.

7. The Founding of Rome; 753 BC (Livy 1.6.4–1.7.3; Plutarch, *Life of Romulus* 9.4–11.3; Ovid, *Fasti* 4.807–862)

As both Romulus and Remus cannot be king of the new city, auspices are taken to determine who will rule.

The taking of auspices entails the marking out of a sacred space from within which an augur observes the flight of birds in order to determine if an action is sanctioned by the gods.

Remus watches from the Aventine Hill.

Remus observes six vultures in flight.

Romulus watches from the Palatine Hill.

Romulus then observes twelve vultures in flight.

Each bother lays claim to the throne.

Romulus kills Remus.

According to one tradition, there is an immediate fight between the two brothers and their followers.

MAP

‘Sites of Rome’

Sites built, finished or refinished between 30 BC and AD 14 and those particularly associated with the Augustan programme of architectural and moral renewal are indicated in CAPITALS.

01. MAUSOLEUM OF AUGUSTUS
02. HOROLOGIUM OF AUGUSTUS
03. ARA PACIS AUGUSTAE (ALTAR OF AUGUSTAN PEACE)
04. Gardens of Lucullus
05. Temple of Flora
06. Temple of Venus Erycina (of Eryx)
07. Gardens of Sallust
08. Precinct of Fortuna ad Portam Collinam
09. Temple of Quirinus
10. Temple of Juno Lucina
11. PORTICUS LIVIAE
12. MONUMENTAL ARCHES OF AUGUSTUS
13. GARDENS OF MAECENAS AND AUDITORIUM
14. Temple of Tellus (conjectural identification)
15. ARCH OF DOLABELLA
16. Temple of Camenae (location uncertain)
17. TEMPLE OF HONOS ET VIRTUS (with ALTAR OF FOR TUNA REDUX)
18. TEMPLE OF BONA DEA SUBSAXANA
19. Scipionic Monuments
    a. Temple of Tempestates (location uncertain
    b. Tomb of the Scipios
20. Pyramid of C. Cestius
21. Porticus Aemilia
22. Grove of Furrina
23. NAUMACHIA OF AUGUSTUS (dimensions uncertain)
24. ARA DITIS PATRIS ET PROSERPINAE (ALTAR OF DIS AND PROSERPINA)

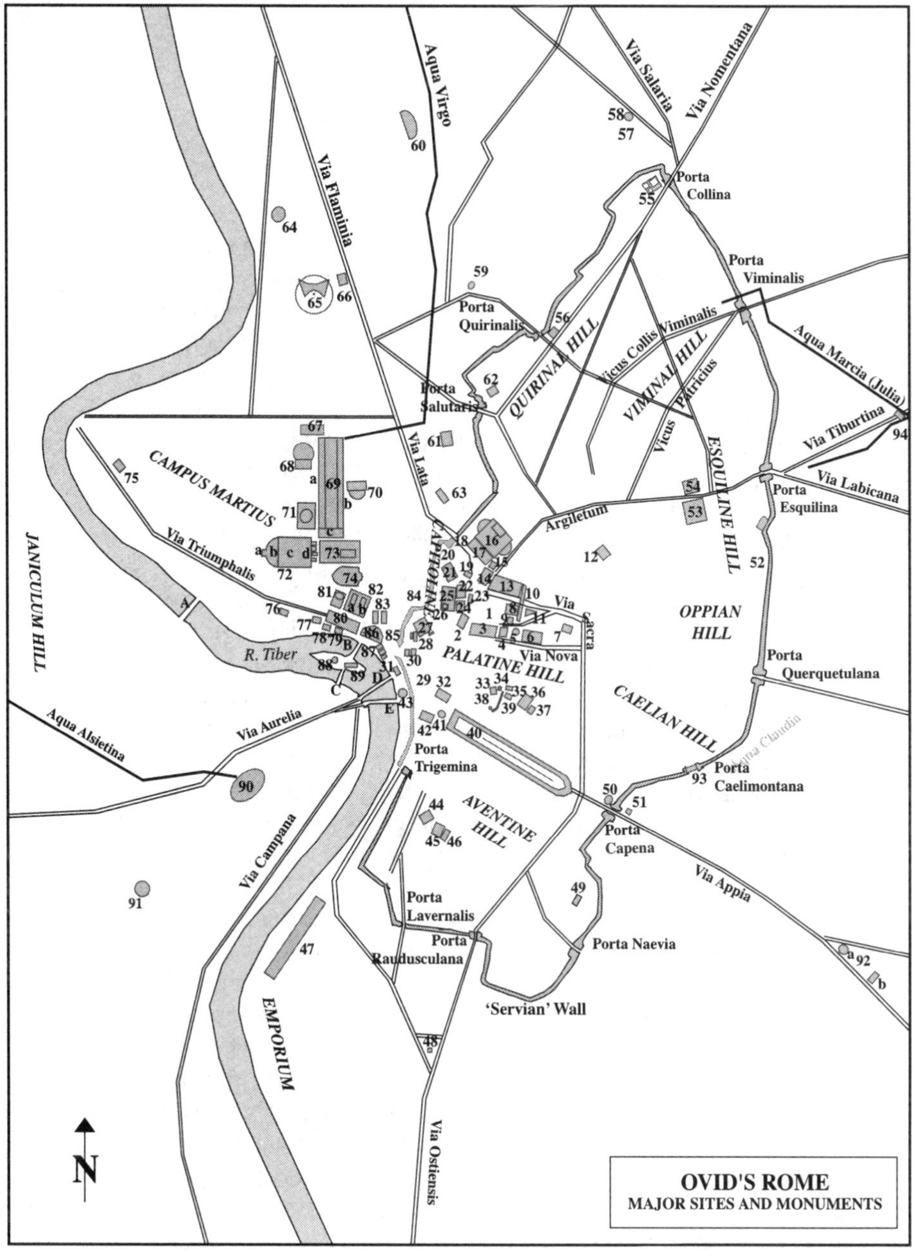

Map 3–1 The Sites of Rome. (Courtesy of Joseph Smith)

25. BASILICA NEPTUNI
26. PANTHEON
27. SAEPTA JULIA
    a. PORTICUS ARGONAUTARUM
    b. PORTICUS MELEAGRI
    c. DIRIBITORIUM
28. Temples of Isis and Serapis
29. BATHS OF AGRIPPA
30. Theatre of Pompey
    a. Temple of Venus Victrix
    b. Theatre
    c. Porticus
    d. Republican Victory temples
31. Porticus Minucia Vetus enclosing the Temple of Lares Permarini (conjectural identification of both porticus and temple)
32. Theatre of Balbus with cryptoporticus
33. Temple of Mars (or Neptune? – conjectural identification)
34. Temple of Hercules Custos (location at west end of Circus uncertain)
35. Temple of Castor and Pollux
36. Temple of Neptune (location on Circus uncertain)
37. Circus Flaminius
38. PORTICUS PHILIPPI enclosing the TEMPLE OF HERCULES MUSARUM
39. PORTICUS OCTAVIAE enclosing
    a. Temple of Juno Regina
    b. Temple of Jupiter Stator
40. Temples of Apollo Sosianus (west) and Bellona (east)
41. Tarpeian Rock
42. Forum Holitorium
43. THEATRE OF MARCELLUS
44. Republican temples of Janus, Juno Sospita and Spes (assignment of names to temples conjectural)
45. Temple of Vedjovis (identified as Jupiter in *Fasti*, its location on Tiber Island is uncertain)
46. Temple of Aesculapius
47. Forum Romanum
48. Temple of Saturn
49. BASILICA JULIA
50. Temple of Castor (and Pollux)
51. Temple of Vesta
52. House of the Vestals
53. Temple of Jupiter Stator
54. TEMPLE OF DIVUS JULIUS
55. ARCH OF AUGUSTUS
56. PORTICUS JULIA and PORTICUS GAII ET LUCII
57. Regia
58. BASILICA AEMILIA
59. CURIA
60. CHALCIDICUM
61. FORUM OF AUGUSTUS enclosing TEMPLE OF MARS ULTOR
62. FORUM OF JULIUS CAESAR enclosing the TEMPLE OF VENUS GENETRIX
63. Clivus Argentarius to the Comitium
64. Temple of Janus Geminus (location uncertain)
65. Arx
66. Temple of Juno Moneta
67. TEMPLE OF CONCORDIA
68. ROSTRA and GOLDEN MILESTONE
69. Porticus Deorum Consentium
70. Tabularium
71. Temple of Vedjovis
72. Temple of Jupiter Optimus Maximus
73. Attendant temples of JUPITER TONANS, Fortuna Primigenia, Mens, Fides and Ops
74. Forum Boarium
75. Temples of Fortuna and Mater Matuta
76. Temple of Portunus
77. Ara Maxima (location uncertain)
78. TEMPLE OF CYBELE (Magna Mater)
79. TEMPLE OF VICTORIA
80. 'HOUSE OF LIVIA' (north) and HOUSE OF AUGUSTUS (south)
81. TEMPLE OF PALATINE APOLLO
82. LIBRARY OF PALATINE APOLLO
83. Lupercal
84. Scalae Caci and Casa Romuli
85. Circus Maximus
86. Temple of Hercules Victor
87. Temple of Ceres, Liber and Libera
88. Temple of Hercules Invictus (conjectural identification)
89. Temple of Minerva
90. Temple of Diana
91. TEMPLE OF JUNO REGINA (location uncertain)
92. Temple of Serapis
93. Temple of Semo Sancus Dius Fidius (location uncertain)
94. Hall of Liberty
    A. PONS AGRIPPAE
    B. PONS FABRICIUS
    C. Pons Cestius
    D. Pons Aemilius
    E. Pons Sublicius

Map 3–1 (*continued*)

The more common tradition is that Romulus first begins to build his city walls on the Palatine.

Remus scornfully jumps over the walls while they are still low.

Remus is then killed by Romulus or by Celer, whom Romulus has placed in charge of the walls.

8. Rome's first kings

Romulus (Livy 1.8.4–1.16.8; Plutarch, *Life of Romulus* 14.1–29.7)

In order to populate Rome, Romulus opens a sanctuary on the Capitoline Hill.

Fugitives from the surrounding regions flee to the Capitoline for asylum.

The gender of Rome's population is thus chiefly male.

Romulus petitions neighboring peoples for women, but without success.

Romulus schemes to obtain women for Rome.

Romulus plans a great celebration for the Summer Consualia.

Romulus sends word of the festivities to the neighboring peoples.

Many people come, especially the Sabines.

The historical Sabines lived in villages northeast of Rome.

During the celebration, Roman men rush out and abduct many of the young Sabine women.

The consequence of the abductions will be war with the Sabines.

The Sabine War

The Sabine forces are led by the king Titus Tatius, of the Sabine city of Cures.

In an early action, the army of Caenina is easily defeated by the Romans.

Romulus kills Acro, king of Caenina, and captures the city.

Romulus offers Acro's armor to Jupiter Feretrius upon the Capitoline and marks out a sacred precinct for the god on that hill.

Following Roman victories over other cities, the Sabines attack Rome.

The Sabines are assisted by a Roman traitor, Tarpeia, daughter of the commander of the Roman forces on the Capitoline Hill.

Tarpeia lusts after the gold jewelry worn by the Sabine warriors.

The warriors wear golden bracelets on their left arms.

The Sabines are a wealthy people famed for their gold.

Tarpeia agrees to let the Sabine army enter the Capitoline walls in exchange for "what they wear on their left arms."

The Sabine army enters by night and destroys the Romans on the Capitoline.

The Sabines repay Tarpeia by crushing her beneath the weight of their shields, which they also wear on their left arms.

Following the capture of the Capitoline, the Sabines attack Romulus and the remaining Romans on the Palatine.

The armies battle in the marshy valley between the two hills.

This valley will eventually be drained and become the Roman Forum.

When the Sabines begin to rout the Romans, Romulus calls upon Jupiter Stator and vows a temple to the god if he will keep the Romans from defeat.

The abducted Sabine women, now Roman mothers, have been watching the slaughter.

Unable to bear it any longer, the women rush onto the battlefield with their infants, position themselves between the armies, and beg their fathers, brothers, and husbands to stop fighting and killing one another.

Peace ensues and the Sabines move to Rome.

Titus Tatius becomes co-regent with Romulus.

Some years later, Titus Tatius is killed.

Later still, after several successful military campaigns, Romulus disappears in a storm while reviewing his army on the Campus Martius.

In disappearing, Romulus was said to have been transformed into the god Quirinus.

Romulus/Quirinus appears to a Roman man, Proculus Julius, and reveals to him the story of his transformation.

Numa Pompilius (Livy 1.17.1–1.21.5; Plutarch, *Life of Numa* 1.1–22.7)

The Roman senate chooses a Sabine, Numa Pompilius, to be Rome's next king.

Numa is famed for his piety and his commitment to justice.

Numa is reluctant to accept the throne.

Numa specifies that auspices must first be taken to reveal the divine will in this matter.

The augur receives a sighting that confirms Numa's selection as being Jupiter's will.

Numa's long reign is marked by peace.

Conspicuously unlike Romulus, Numa does not take Rome to war.

Numa regulates the Roman calendar, appointing sacred days and days for business.

According to Livy, Numa establishes many priestly offices:

- The Major Flamens
- The Vestal Virgins
- The Salii

  The Salii are priests of Mars.

  During the month of March, they dance around Rome, wearing archaic warrior dress and singing ancient songs.

  At first there were twelve; later their number was increased to twenty-four.

- The Pontifices

  The Pontifices are the priests in charge of the Roman state religion.

  The Pontifices are in charge of the Roman calendar as well.

  Latin *Pontifex* means 'bridge builder'.

  The Pontifices are, in fact, associated with a bridge, the Pons Sublicius.

  The Pons Sublicius is a sacred wooden bridge, the oldest bridge in Rome.

  When repairs are required, those are accompanied by pontifical rites.

  A term comparable to Latin *Pontifex* occurs in India (Dumézil 1996).

  Sanskrit *pathi-kṛt* means 'path maker'.

  Sanskrit *pathi-* and Latin *ponti-* are of common Indo-European origin.

  Sanskrit *-kṛt* and Latin *-fex* are not cognate, but have the same meaning.

  Sanskrit *pathi-kṛt* is an epithet used of gods and priests.

  Latin *Pontifex* likely has (in origin) the sense of 'path maker' and refers to the sacred actions of the priest.

  The Pontifex Maximus

  The Pontifex Maximus is the chief of the Pontifices.

The Pontifex Maximus appoints and supervises the Vestal Virgins.

The Pontifex Maximus appoints the Flamens and the Rex Sacrorum.

During the period of the Roman monarchy, the king had certain religious duties.

When the monarchy was abolished (509 BC), it seems, a new priestly office was created, that of the Rex Sacrorum.

The Rex Sacrorum continues to perform the sacred duties that had belonged to the king.

The wife of the Rex Sacrorum, the Regina Sacrorum, also performs certain sacred duties.

Numa dedicates an altar to Jupiter Elicius on the Aventine Hill.

Numa establishes sacrifices, such as that to Fides ('Good Faith').

Once a year, the (Major) Flamens ride to the shrine of Fides in a covered carriage drawn by two horses.

There they sacrifice to Fides with their right hands covered with a white cloth up to their fingers.

Egeria is the wife of Numa.

Egeria is a nymph who provides Numa with much of his wisdom.

During the reign of Numa, Jupiter causes the *ancile* to fall to Rome from heaven.

The *ancile* is a shield of an archaic figure-8 shape.

The *ancile* would bring sovereignty to the one who possessed it.

Numa, therefore, orders that eleven copies of the *ancile* be made to minimize the possibility of the shield being stolen.

Mamurius Veturius is the craftsman who makes the duplicate shields.

Numa keeps the shields in his residence, the Regia.

In a later time, the Regia becomes the headquarters of the Pontifex Maximus.

The Salii carry the twelve shields as they leap and dance around Rome during the month of March.

After forty-three years as king, Numa dies.

Tullus Hostilius (Livy 1.22.1–1.31.8; Dionysius of Halicarnassus 3.1.1–3.35.6)

The third king of Rome, Tullus Hostilius, returns Rome to war-making.

Rome goes to war with Alba Longa.

- The war with Alba Longa will be decided by a fight between three warriors from each city.
    - The Horatii, triplet brothers, fight for Rome.
    - The Curiatii, triplet brothers, fight for Alba Longa.
    - The two sets of triplets are related as cousins.
- Horatius
    - After two of the Roman warriors are killed, the surviving third brother Horatius slays the three Curiatii.
    - The Roman people greet Horatius as a hero.
    - Horatia, his sister, grieves when she sees him.
        - One of the slain Curiatii was her lover.
    - Horatius kills Horatia.
        - Horatius is tried and convicted in the murder of his sister.
        - The verdict is overturned upon appeal to the populace.
    - Horatius still must be cleansed of the bloodguilt of the murder.
        - His family administers a cleansing ritual.
            - Sacrifices are offered to Juno Sororia and Janus Curiatius.
            - With his head veiled, Horatius passes beneath a wooden beam that spans a street.
                - The beam is called the *Tigillum Sororium* ('Sister's Beam').
                - The rite continued to be used in Rome under the administration of the family Horatii.

Mettius Fuffetius

- The Alban dictator, Mettius Fuffetius, is now compelled to be an unwilling ally of Rome.
- Mettius treacherously withdraws his forces from a battle fought against the armies of Fidenae and Veii.
    - Mettius intends to rejoin the battle when he sees who will be the victor.
- The Roman flank is disastrously exposed.
- Tullus Hostilius responds by maneuvering his troops and making vows to the gods Quirinus, Ops, and Saturnus.
- The Roman army is victorious.
- Tullus Hostilius pretends he does not know of the treachery of Mettius Fuffetius.
- The next day, Tullus Hostilius seizes an unsuspecting Mettius and orders his execution.

Mettius is chained to two four-horse chariots and dismembered as the chariots race in different directions.

Sometime later, a plague comes upon Rome.

Tullus attempts to perform rites to Jupiter Elicius that Numa had performed.

Tullus does not know the proper procedure, however.

Jupiter strikes Tullus with lightning, and Tullus dies.

Ancus Marcius (Livy 1.32.1–1.34.12; Dionysius of Halicarnassus 3.36.1–3.48.4)

The fourth king of Rome, Ancus Marcius, is a grandson of Numa Pompilius.

Ancus Marcius brings wealth to Rome from spoils of war.

Ancus builds the Pons Sublicius, the sacred bridge associated with the Pontifices.

During the reign of Ancus, Tarquinius Priscus from the Etruscan city of Tarquinii settles in Rome and rises to a position of prominence.

9. The Tarquin kings (Livy 1.35.1–60.4)

After the death of Ancus Marcius, Tarquinius Priscus becomes king.

Tarquinius Priscus (Tarquin the Elder) is fifth king of Rome.

Tarquinius Priscus lays the foundations for the Capitoline temple of Jupiter Optimus Maximus.

Tarquinius marries his daughter to Servius Tullius.

Servius Tullius was born the son of a slave in the household of Tarquinius.

Tarquinius raised Servius as his adopted son.

The two sons of Ancus Marcius cause Tarquinius Priscus to be murdered.

Servius Tullius succeeds Tarquinius Priscus as the sixth king of Rome.

Because of his own great fortune at being adopted by Tarquinius Priscus, Servius is especially devoted to the goddess Fortuna.

Tarquinius Superbus, son of Tarquinius Priscus, and his wife Tullia, daughter of Servius Tullius, murder Servius.

Tarquinius Superbus succeeds Servius Tullius as the seventh and final king of Rome.

10. A Roman mythic history (Dumézil 1996, 1988)

Dumézil argues that in Rome, inherited Indo-European mythic traditions have been transposed into historical narrative.

The history of early Rome is a mythic history.

Elements of (pseudo-) historical Roman tradition have been wed to identifiable mythic motifs of primitive Indo-European origin.

Romulus and Remus

- Romulus and Remus are the Roman homologues of the broadly attested Indo-European divine twins.
  - A well-known example is that of the Aśvins of India.
  - The Aśvins belong to the third function of divine society.
  - Similarly, Romulus and Remus were raised as shepherds (third-function occupation).
- Romulus is a more complex figure.
  - Romulus is transfunctional: he spans the three Indo-European functions.
    - At crucial moments in his life, Romulus is affiliated with each of the three gods of the Pre-Capitoline triad.
      - Romulus is the son of Mars.
      - Romulus calls upon Jupiter when his army is about to be routed by the Sabines.
      - Romulus is transformed into Quirinus at the end of his life.
- Following the murder of Remus, however, Romulus's principal role in the Roman mythic history is that of sovereign.
  - Romulus is Rome's founding king.
  - Romulus embodies the first function.

The Sabines

- In Rome's mythic history, the Sabines provide the means of fertility that will ensure the survival of Rome (the Sabine women).
- The Sabines are a wealthy people.
  - The Sabines possess fabulous golden bracelets and jeweled rings.
- The Sabines embody the third function: the realm of wealth, fertility, sensuality.
  - Varro (*Ling.* 5.74) preserves a list of the gods that Titus Tatius, the Sabine king, introduced to Rome:
    - Ops, Flora, Vediovis, Saturnus, Sol, Luna, Volcanus, Summanus, Larunda, Terminus, Quirinus, Vortumnus, the Lares, Diana, and Lucina
    - The third-function god Quirinus is notably present and the others can be reasonably associated with third-function ideas.

The Sabine War

- The war between Romulus and the Sabines is the Roman reflex of a primitive Indo-European tradition about a conflict between the functions: first/second function vs. third function.
  - Well-preserved reflexes of the tradition are also found in India, Scandinavia, and Ireland.
  - These conflicts are set in a time in which divine society is undergoing its full formation.

Two opposing sets of gods, following a confrontation, are merged into one.

In Rome, where myth is transposed into historical narrative, the opposing parties belong to human, rather than divine, society.

Romulus (sovereign; son of the warrior god Mars) wages nascent Rome's war against the Sabines (possessors of wealth and means of fertility).

After cessation of fighting, the Sabines move to Rome and merge with Romulus's population.

Numa Pompilius

Like Romulus, Rome's second king, the Sabine Numa Pompilius, embodies the first function in Rome's mythic history.

Numa brings order and justice to Romulus's Rome, continuing the process of molding the young city.

Romulus and Numa constitute an antithetical pair.

Romulus is violent and has a life charged with magic.

- Romulus kills Remus in order to be king.
- Romulus settles Rome with criminals.
- Romulus takes Rome to war.
- Romulus seizes lands from other peoples and expands Rome's geography.
- Romulus has a supernatural conception and is miraculously saved when Amulius exposes him.
- Romulus is rescued by Jupiter's intervention at a crucial moment in battle.
- Romulus is transformed into a god at the end of his life.

Numa is peaceful.

- Numa enjoys a life of quiet contemplation.
- Numa must be persuaded to take the throne.
- Numa is devoted to the goddess Fides ('Good Faith').
- Numa establishes sacred festivals and holy offices.
- Numa brings order and justice to Rome.
- Numa builds the first temple to Terminus, god of boundaries, and makes boundaries between Rome and its neighbors and within Rome sacrosanct.
- Numa has a natural birth.
- Numa dies a natural death in old age.

Romulus and Numa represent two different aspects of the Indo-European first function.

Romulus embodies the magical aspect.

Numa embodies the legal aspect.

Tullus Hostilius

In Rome's mythic history, Tullus Hostilius embodies the second function.

Under his leadership, Rome goes to war in earnest, beginning with the war with Alba Longa.

That war is settled by the duel between the three Horatii and the three Curiatii.

The number of warriors, three, represents, in the context of an Indo-European ideology, the totality of society.

The three Horatii and the three Curiatii stand as a proxy for all of Roman society and Alban society respectively.

The fury that possesses Horatius and makes him not only a threat to the enemy (the Curiatii) but also to his own people (Horatia) is typical of the warrior madness that grips the Indo-European warrior.

Bibliography and Further Reading

Adkins, Lesley, and Roy Adkins. 1996. *Dictionary of Roman Religion.* Oxford: Oxford University Press.

Beard, Mary, John North, and Simon Price. 1998. *Religions of Rome.* Cambridge: Cambridge University Press.

Benveniste, Émile. 1969. *Le vocabulaire des institutions indo-européennes.* Paris: Les Éditions de Minuit.

Boyle, Anthony, and Roger Woodard. 2004. *Ovid: Fasti.* Revised edition. London: Penguin Books.

Dumézil, Georges. 1996. *Archaic Roman Religion.* Reprint edition. Baltimore: Johns Hopkins University Press.

_____. 1988. *Mitra-Varuna.* Reprint edition. New York: Zone Books.

_____. 1935. *Flamen-Brahman.* Paris: Paul Geuthner.

Grimal, Pierre. 1997. *The Dictionary of Classical Mythology.* Oxford: Blackwell.

Rix, Helmut. 2004. "Etruscan." In Roger Woodard, *The Cambridge Encyclopedia of the World's Ancient Languages*, pp. 943–966. Cambridge: Cambridge University Press.

Scheid, John. 2003. *An Introduction to Roman Religion.* Bloomington and Indianapolis: University of Indiana Press.

Turcan, Robert. 2000. *The Gods of Ancient Rome.* New York: Routledge.

Woolf, Greg. 2003. *Cambridge Illustrated History of the Roman World.* Cambridge: Cambridge University Press.

4 The Greeks and Their Gods

Outline of Key Terms and Concepts

1. Indo-Europeans in the Balkan Peninsula

   The Indo-European people who would come to be called the Greeks probably arrived in the Balkan Peninsula in about 2100–1900 BC.

   The Balkan Peninsula was inhabited at the time of their arrival.

   Some evidence suggests the presence of Luvians, an Indo-European people, in the Balkan Peninsula prior to the arrival of the Greeks (Palmer 1996; 1963).

2. The Mycenaean Greeks

   The earliest Greek civilization to leave behind written records is that of the Mycenaean Greeks (1600–1100 BC).

   The Mycenaeans are the Greeks whom Homer (eighth century BC) envisions in his epic poems about the Trojan War:

   - *The Iliad:* the tale of the tenth and final year of the war with Troy
   - *The Odyssey:* the tale of the return of Odysseus from the war to his home in Ithaca

   The Mycenaean Greeks wrote with the script that scholars call "Linear B."

   The British archaeologist Sir Arthur Evans began to excavate the ancient site of Knossos (on Crete) in 1900.

   Evans unearthed a large number of clay tablets from the site.

   Evans gave the name "Linear B" to the script of one set of tablets.

   Evans named the script of another set of tablets "Linear A," and called that of a third set "Hieroglyphic."

   Linear B was deciphered by Michael Ventris, a British architect and amateur philologist, in 1952.

   Linear B is not an alphabet, but a syllabic script.

   Each symbol of the script represents a syllable (rather than a single consonant or vowel, as in an alphabet).

   For example, *korwa* 'girl' is spelled with two symbols: *ko-wa*.

The majority of Linear B tablets have been found at the sites of Knossos, Pylos, Mycenae, and Thebes.

The Linear B tablets date from about 1400 to 1200 BC.

The Linear B tablets are primarily various types of accounting documents:

lists of personal names; livestock and agricultural records; land use and ownership records; lists of tribute and ritual offerings; inventories of textiles and furnishings; inventories of military equipment.

Even so, the Linear B documents contain the names of most of the major Greek gods known from later periods of Greek culture:

- Zeus (= Roman Jupiter)
- Hera (= Roman Juno)
- Demeter (= Roman Ceres)

  The divine name "Demeter" does not itself occur in the Linear B documents, but the term *Potnia* 'mistress' may well be a reference to her.

  The term is used to denote Demeter and her daughter Persephone in later periods.

  The term is also used to refer to other female deities in later periods.

  In the Mycenaean documents, reference is made to Athena Potnia.

- Poseidon (= Roman Neptune)
- Hephaestus (= Roman Vulcan)

  The god's name is attested only by a man's name, Haphaistios, which is derived from the divine name.

- Ares (= Roman Mars)
- Athena (= Roman Minerva)
- Paean (Apollo)

  In the Linear B documents, the name "Apollo" does not occur, but this god may very well be the deity who is denoted by the term *Paean*, meaning 'healer', Apollo's common epithet in later periods.

- Artemis (= Roman Diana)
- Hermes (= Roman Mercury)
- Dionysus (= Roman Bacchus)

The single major Greek deity to whom there is no reference is the goddess Aphrodite (= Roman Venus).

Her absence from the Mycenaean records might be an accidental gap.

On the other hand, her absence may reveal that Aphrodite had not yet become part of the Greek pantheon.

The Greeks probably borrowed Aphrodite from the Phoenicians.

The Phoenician source-deity is the fertility goddess Astarte.

The Linear B documents also contain the names of some minor Greek gods known from later periods:

- Eileithyia

A goddess of childbirth

- Erinys

A goddess (often in the plural) who brings retribution for crimes, especially for crimes against family members

A name sometimes associated with Demeter

The Linear B documents also preserve the names of Greek deities who are not known from later periods.

3. The Greek "Dark Age" (1100–750 BC)

The Mycenaean Greek civilization comes to an end in about 1100 BC.

Writing ceases to be attested in Greece.

The eclipsing of the Mycenaeans is but one of a set of catastrophic events that sweep across the eastern Mediterranean at this time.

In Anatolia, the powerful Hittite civilization comes to an end.

The prosperous trading center and cosmopolitan city of Ugarit on the coast of Syria is destroyed.

The Egyptians report a desperate fight against a powerful enemy, whom they are able to defeat.

In Egyptian records, this enemy is referred to as the "people of the land and sea."

Scholars commonly use the term Sea Peoples to refer to this group.

With the approaching end of the Mycenaean civilization, many Greeks leave the mainland for Cyprus, where there is already a Greek community.

In Cyprus, the Mycenaean Greek émigrés preserve much of their culture.

Cyprus thus escapes the Greek Dark Age.

The Cypriot Greeks develop a new syllabic script that is quite similar to Linear B in its spelling practices.

The script is called the Cypriot Syllabary.

Phoenicians also settle on Cyprus.

Greek-Phoenician interaction on Cyprus may be the source of important developments in Greek culture.

The Greek alphabet perhaps takes shape on Cyprus in this period.

The Greek alphabet is based on the Phoenician consonantal script.

A consonantal script is one that represents only consonants, not vowels.

The Greeks adapt the Phoenician script for Greek use by assigning vowel values to some of the unneeded consonantal symbols.

In this time and place, the Greeks may also have acquired mythic traditions from the Phoenicians.

In contrast to the Romans, the Greeks appear to have given up many of their ancestral Indo-European traditions.

The cultures of the ancient Near East exert significant influence upon the Greeks.

Bibliography and Further Reading

Chadwick, John. 1989. *Linear B and Related Scripts.* Berkeley and Los Angeles: University of California Press.

_____. 1967. *The Decipherment of Linear B.* 2nd ed. Cambridge: Cambridge University Press.

Dickenson, Oliver. 1994. *The Aegean Bronze Age.* Cambridge: Cambridge University Press.

Finley, M. I. 1981. *Early Greece.* New York: Norton.

Palmer, Leonard. 1996. *The Greek Language.* Reprint edition. Norman, Oklahoma: University of Oklahoma Press.

_____. 1963. *Mycenaeans and Minoans.* New York: Alfred A. Knopf.

Pomeroy, Sarah et al. 1999. *Ancient Greece.* Oxford: Oxford University Press.

Robinson, Andrew. 2002. *Lost Languages.* New York: McGraw-Hill.

Ventris, Michael, and John Chadwick. 1973. *Documents in Mycenaean Greek.* 2nd ed. Cambridge: Cambridge University Press.

Woodard, Roger. 2003. "Writing Systems." In B. Comrie, S. Matthews, and M. Polinsky, *The Atlas of Languages*, revised edition, pp. 160–207. London: Quarto.

_____. 1997a. *Greek Writing from Knossos to Homer.* Oxford: Oxford University Press.

_____. 1997b. "Linguistic Connections Between Greeks and Non-Greeks." In J. Coleman and C. Walz, *Greeks and Barbarians*, pp. 29–60. Baltimore: CDL.

5 Hesiod's Theogony

Outline of Key Terms and Concepts

1. The Greek poet Hesiod (eighth century BC) presents the tale of the creation of the cosmos in his epic poem, the *Theogony*.

   The beginning of things (*Theogony* 116–132)

   At the beginning, Chaos, a great void, came into existence.

   Next appeared:

   - Gaea ('Earth')
   - Tartarus, a dim place in the depths of earth
   - Eros ('Desire')

   Gaea, the Earth, gives birth to three beings:

   - Uranus ('Sky')
   - Urea ('Mountains')
   - Pontus ('Sea')

   These are all fatherless conceptions.

   Gaea takes Uranus as her consort.

2. The offspring of Gaea and Uranus (*Theogony* 132–156)

   With Uranus, Gaea conceives the twelve Titans.

   First, five sons are born.

   Oceanus, Coeus, Crius, Hyperion, Iapetus

   Next, six daughters are born.

   Theia, Rhea, Themis, Mnemosyne, Phoebe, Tethys

   Finally, a sixth son is born.

   Cronus

   Gaea and Uranus then produce the three Cyclopes.

   Brontes, Steropes, Arges

   The Cyclopes each have a single eye in the middle of their foreheads.

   They are craftsmen who fashion the thunder and thunderbolt.

   Gaea and Uranus also produce the three Hecatoncheires.

   Cottus, Briareus, Gyes

   The Hecatoncheires each have one hundred arms and fifty heads.

   They are creatures of gargantuan strength.

3. In time, many of the Titans will couple and produce offspring.

   The offspring of Oceanus and Tethys (*Theogony* 337–370):

   - The 3,000 rivers of the world
   - The 3,000 Oceanids (ocean nymphs)

   The offspring of Iapetus and Clymene, one of the Oceanids (*Theogony* 507–525):

   - Atlas

     Atlas supports the heavens upon his shoulders.

     This is a punishment imposed on Atlas by Zeus.

   - Menoetius

     Menoetius is full of pride; for that, Zeus strikes him down with a thunderbolt.

   - Prometheus

     Prometheus steals fire and gives it to men (*Theogony* 561–569).

     Zeus is angry and punishes men by creating the first woman (*Theogony* 570–602).

   - Epimetheus

     Epimetheus is recipient of the first woman.

   The offspring of Hyperion and Theia (*Theogony* 371–374):

   - Helios: the sun
   - Selene: the moon
   - Eos: the dawn

   The offspring of Coeus and Phoebe (*Theogony* 404–410):

   - Leto

     Leto will become one of Zeus's wives.

   - Asteria

     Asteria will give birth to the daughter Hecate (*Theogony* 411–452).

     For Hesiod, Hecate is a goddess who is kindly disposed toward humans and helps them in various ways.

     Later, Hecate becomes associated with the netherworld and sorcery.

   The offspring of Crius and Eurybia, a daughter of Gaea and Pontus (*Theogony* 375–403):

   - Pallas

     Pallas will become the husband of the river Styx, the oldest of the daughters of Oceanus.

     Styx flows through the realm of Hades (*Theogony* 775–806)

     The gods swear their oaths by water from the river Styx.

- Perses

  Perses will marry Asteria, and so will father Hecate.

- Astraeus

  Astraeus will marry Eos.

  Among the offspring of Astraeus and Eos are the winds:

  Zephyrus: the West Wind

  Boreas: the North Wind

  Notus: the South Wind

The offspring of Mnemosyne and Zeus (*Theogony* 75–103):

The Muses, the nine goddesses of artistic inspiration

4. Gaea, Uranus, and Cronus (*Theogony* 156–210)

As his children are born, Uranus hides them away in a secret place in the Earth.

Gaea grows weary from the burden and asks her children to help her.

Cronus alone is willing to help.

Gaea hides Cronus in a place of ambush and gives him a jagged sickle of adamant that she has made.

Uranus comes to Gaea and prepares to make love to her.

Cronus springs up from his hiding place, and with the sickle, he castrates his father Uranus.

Gaea conceives children by the blood that flows from the wound of Uranus.

The Erinyes (the Furies): spirits who avenge crimes, especially those committed against family members

Giants with armor and great spears

The Meliae: nymphs of the ash tree

Cronus throws his father's genitals into the sea.

Aphrodite is born from the genitals floating in the sea.

5. Rhea and Cronus (*Theogony* 453–506)

Cronus takes Rhea as his consort.

Five children are borne to Cronus by Rhea:

- Hestia: goddess of the hearth
- Demeter: goddess of grain
- Hera: goddess of women
- Hades: god of the netherworld
- Poseidon: god of the sea

As each child is born, Cronus swallows the child.

Gaea and Uranus have warned Cronus that one of his own children will overthrow him.

Rhea, pregnant with a sixth child, asks Gaea and Uranus to devise a scheme for saving the child.

Gaea and Uranus send Rhea to Crete, where she gives birth to Zeus.

Gaea hides Zeus in a cave beneath Mt. Aegeum.

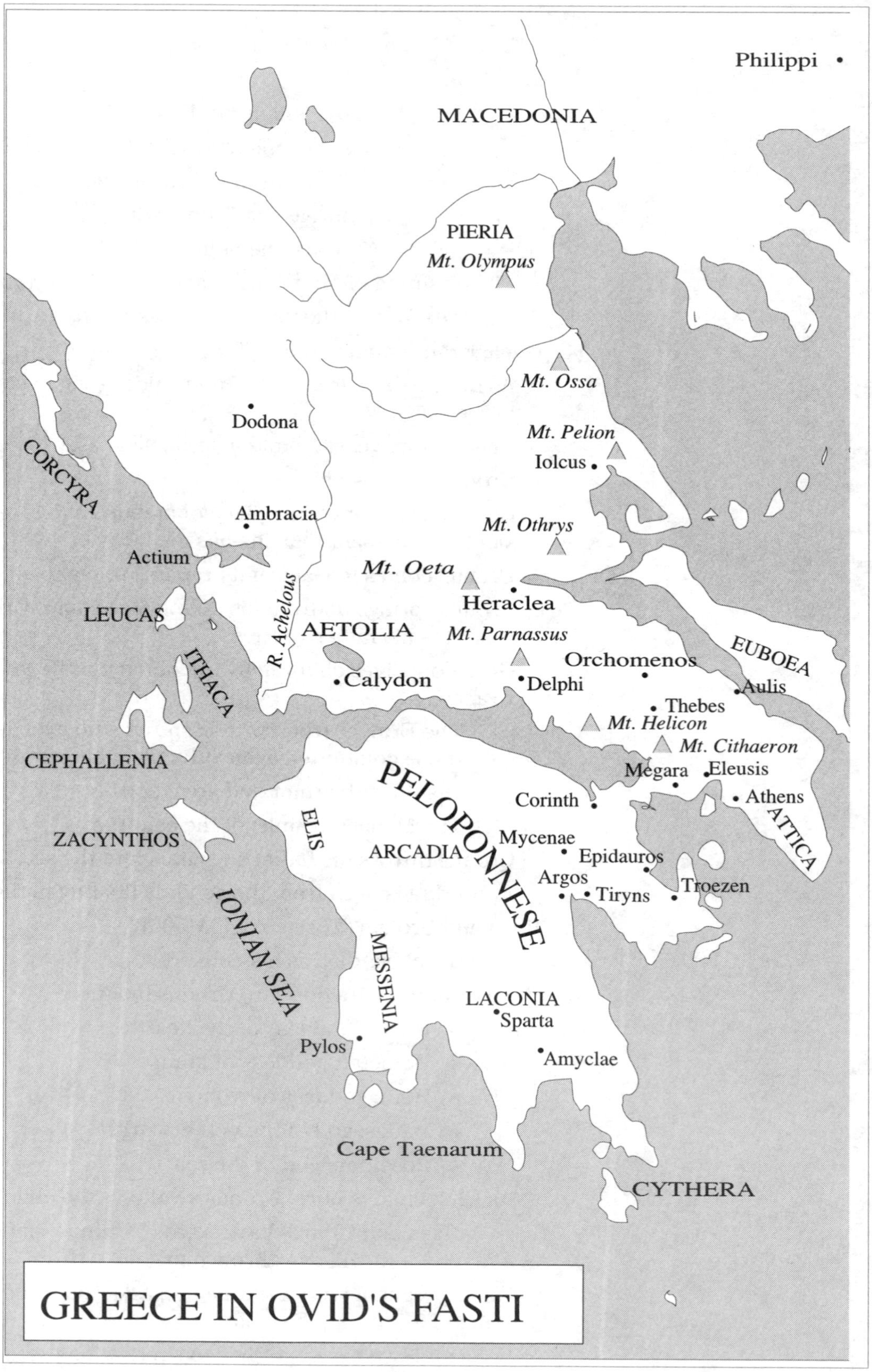

Map 5–1 Early Greece (courtesy of Joseph Smith)

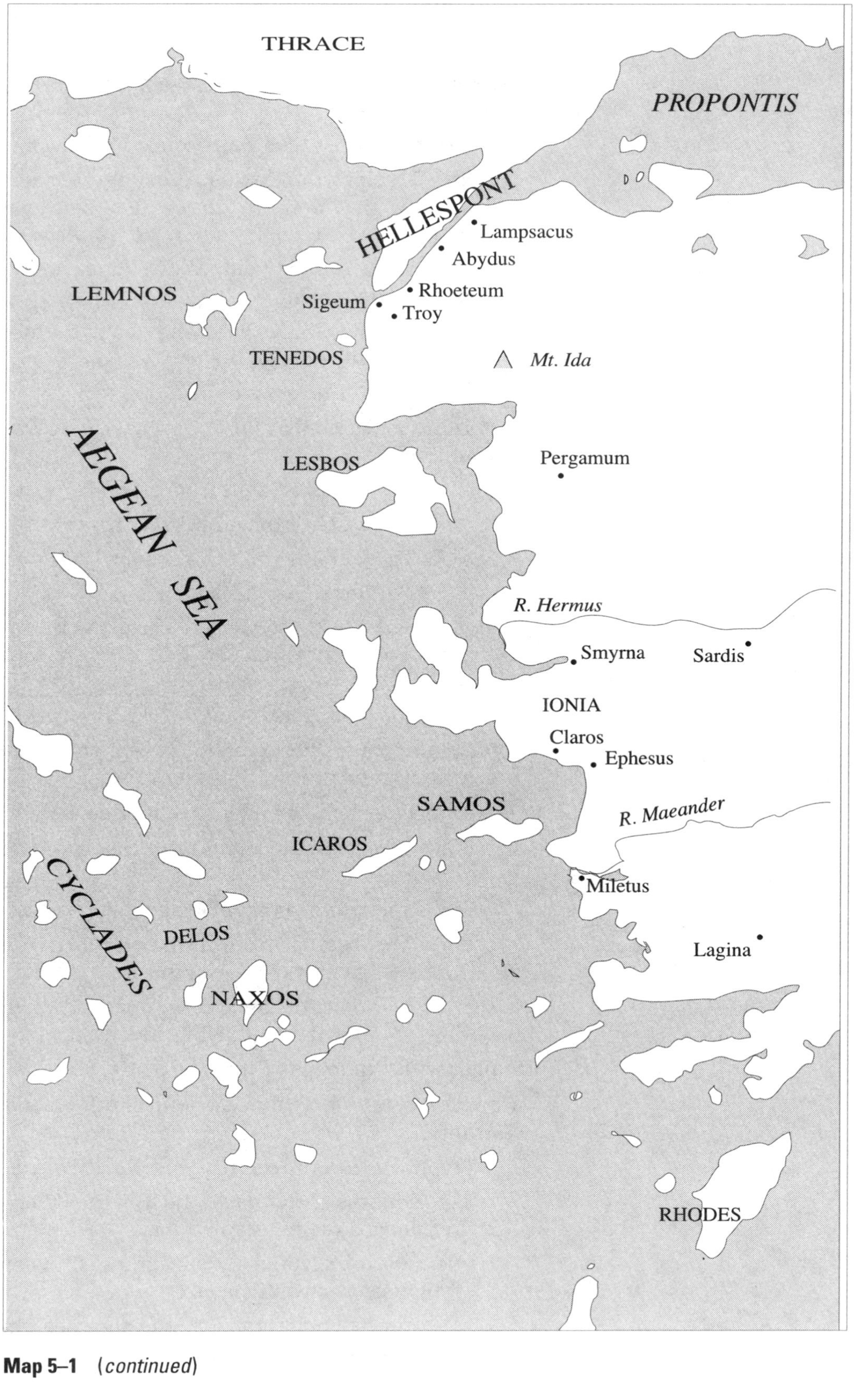

Map 5–1 (*continued*)

Gaea presents a stone wrapped in baby's clothing to Cronus.

Cronus swallows the stone.

After Zeus has grown up, Cronus regurgitates the stone and his five other children.

Hesiod says Cronus was tricked by Gaea into doing so.

The Greek mythographer Apollodorus (second century BC or AD) says that Metis, the first wife of Zeus, gave Cronus a drug that caused the regurgitation (*Bibliotheca* 1.2.1).

Zeus then releases the Cyclopes, who have not yet been freed from Uranus's imprisonment.

The Cyclopes thank Zeus by giving to him thunder and thunderbolt, the characteristic weapon of the sky-god.

6. The Titanomachy (*Theogony* 617–735)

The Titans and the children of Cronus, led by Zeus, go to war with one another.

Zeus and his allies fight from atop Mt. Olympus.

The Titans fight from atop Mt. Othrys.

The war goes on for ten years.

Neither side gains an advantage.

Following Gaea's advice, Zeus releases the Hecatoncheires from their imprisonment within earth.

Agreeing to join the fight on the side of Zeus, the Hecatoncheires lob great stones onto Mt. Othrys.

The fighting intensifies; creation is shaken to the core; Zeus unleashes the full force of his might.

The Titans are defeated and Zeus imprisons them in Tartarus.

Zeus places the Hecatoncheires as the Titans' guards in Tartarus.

Tartarus is a dim place beneath earth.

The distance from earth to Tartarus is the same as the distance from heaven to earth.

That distance is the space through which a bronze anvil would fall for ten days.

7. The fight with Typhoeus (*Theogony* 820–885)

Gaea gives birth to Typhoeus, her last offspring, fathered by Tartarus.

Typhoeus is a dragon with one hundred snake heads.

Apollodorus (*Bibliotheca* 1.6.3) writes that Typhoeus was born in Cilicia, a region of Anatolia.

Nonnus, an Egyptian Greek author (fifth century AD), describes Typhoeus as gigantic in size.

As Typhoeus stands in the deep sea, the waves reach to his waist, and his head crashes into the clouds (*Dionysiaca* 1. 268–271).

Typhoeus comes as a challenge to Zeus's position as king of gods and mortals.

Zeus's fight with Typhoeus is desperate, but pounding the dragon with his thunderbolts, Zeus is victorious and casts Typhoeus into Tartarus.

Apollodorus (*Bibliotheca* 1.6.3) adds other details of Zeus's battle with Typhoeus:

- Zeus wounds Typhoeus with a sickle of adamant and they fight hand-to-hand.
- Typhoeus traps Zeus in his coils, takes away the sickle, and cuts the tendons from Zeus's hands and feet.
- Typhoeus carries Zeus to a cave in Cilicia, where he is guarded by the dragoness Delphyne, and hides the tendons.
- Hermes and Pan, Greek gods, steal the tendons and fit them back into Zeus's hands and feet.
- Zeus attacks and vanquishes Typhoeus, trapping him beneath Mt. Etna in Sicily.

8. The Hittite "kingship-in-heaven" myth

The Hittites are an Indo-European people of Anatolia.

The Hittite civilization extended from the early second millennium BC to about 1200 BC.

Archaeologists have unearthed an enormous quantity of Hittite documents at the site of the ancient Hittite capital of Hattusa.

The Hittites wrote chiefly on clay tablets using a cuneiform writing system.

Cuneiform symbols are characteristically wedge-shaped, hence the name (from Latin *cuneus* 'wedge').

Among the mythological Hittite documents is a set of texts telling the story of a succession of heavenly kings.

Most important are the texts called *The Song of Kumarbi* and *The Song of Ullikummi.*

The Hittite kingship-in-heaven myth offers a close parallel to the Greek story of the rise of Zeus to power.

The Song of Kumarbi

Alalu is the king in heaven.

In the ninth year of Alalu's reign, Anu challenges Alalu for the throne of heaven.

Alalu and Anu fight, and Alalu flees down to the "dark earth."

Anu reigns as king in heaven for nine years.

In the ninth year of Anu's reign, Kumarbi challenges Anu for the throne of heaven.

Kumarbi and Anu fight, and Anu flees like a bird to the sky.

Kumarbi chases Anu and seizes him.

Kumarbi bites off and swallows Anu's genitals.

Anu taunts Kumarbi, telling him that his (Anu's) offspring are now developing within Kumarbi:

- Tesub: the storm-god
- Tasmisu: companion of the storm-god
- Aranzaha: the Tigris River

Anu discusses with his unborn children within Kumarbi how they can exit from Kumarbi's body when the time comes for their birth.

The children are born; the text focuses most attention on the birth of the storm-god, Tesub.

After Tesub is born, he battles Kumarbi.

The text is damaged at this point (and elsewhere), but Tesub must here defeat Kumarbi since he is presented as the reigning king in heaven in the ensuing text.

Hittite-Greek equivalences in the *Song of Kumarbi:*

- Anu = Uranus

Each is emasculated and supplanted by the next heavenly sovereign.

- Kumarbi = Cronus

Each is the emasculator.

Cronus emasculates with a toothed sickle.

Kumarbi emasculates with his own teeth.

Each has gods trapped within his body.

- Tesub = Zeus

Zeus is the sky-god whose weapon is the thunderbolt, and Tesub is the storm-god.

Both the Greek and Hittite accounts focus attention on the birth of the sky/storm-god.

Zeus and Tesub each vanquish the emasculating predecessor and take the throne of heaven.

The Song of Ullikummi

Scheming to recover his throne, Kumarbi engenders an offspring.

Kumarbi has intercourse with a giant rock.

The rock gives birth to a monstrous stone child, Ullikummi.

Kumarbi seeks a caregiver for Ullikummi and mounts him on the right shoulder of Ubelluri.

Ubelluri is an Atlas-like giant who holds up heaven and earth.

On Ubelluri's shoulder, Ullikummi grows at an enormous rate.

On the fifteenth day of his life, Ullikummi is described as standing in the sea like a shaft, with the waves lapping at his waist and his head reaching to heaven.

The sun-god sees the stone giant Ullikummi and tells the gods.

Tesub and Tasmisu go to see Ullikummi for themselves and are overwhelmed with despair.

Ishtar, the fertility goddess, tries to charm Ullikummi with her beauty and with music.

A great wave tells Ishtar that she cannot succeed; the stone giant can neither see nor hear.

The gods prepare for war and go out to meet Ullikummi.

Ullikummi defeats the gods.

Ullikummi continues to grow; he now reaches to the temple of Hebat, Tesub's wife, in heaven.

While in her temple, Hebat could communicate with Tesub.

Hebat now flees her temple.

Tasmisu finds Hebat and tells her of Tesub's fate.

Tasmisu and Tesub go to see Ea, god of wisdom, in Apsu.

Ea takes counsel with Enlil, god of the atmosphere.

Ea goes to see Ubelluri, the giant supporting heaven and earth, and on whose right shoulder Ullikummi has been mounted.

Ea discovers that Ubelluri is unaware of the presence of Ullikummi on his shoulder.

Ea calls upon the "gods of old" to bring out the ancient copper knife that had been used to sever heaven from earth.

With the copper blade, Ullikummi is severed from the shoulder of Ubelluri.

Tesub fights and defeats the dislodged Ullikummi.

Hittite-Greek equivalences in the *Song of Ullikummi:*

- Ullikummi = Typhoeus

Each is a monstrous gigantic creature conceived and birthed expressly to overthrow the storm/sky-god, the reigning king of heaven.

Typhoeus is born from the Earth (Gaea).

Ullikummi is born from a great rock.

The description of fifteen-day-old Ullikummi standing in the sea is remarkably similar to Nonnus' description of Typhoeus standing in the sea.

The late date of Nonnus (fifth century AD) must be kept in mind; Nonnus could have borrowed his description of Typhoeus from an earlier Near Eastern text.

- Copper knife = adamantine sickle (Littleton)

  Each is a cutting blade that was used at an earlier time to sever heaven from earth (in Greek tradition, the castration of Uranus, "Heaven," separated him physically from his consort Gaea "Earth").

  Each blade was subsequently used in overcoming the final challenge to the sovereignty of the storm/sky-god.

9. Is the kingship-in-heaven myth of the Greeks and the Hittites of common Indo-European origin? (Littleton, Puhvel)

The Hittite tradition is linguistically and culturally complex.

The chief deities of the Hittite myth are *not* Hittite gods, but Hurrian gods.

Tesub, Tasmisu, Aranzaha.

The Hurrians are a non-Indo-European people of Anatolia, neighbors to the Hittites.

The Hittites appear to have acquired the myth from the non-Indo-European Hurrians.

Other deities appearing in the Hurrio-Hittite tradition are Mesopotamian gods (and non-Indo-European)—Anu, Ishtar, Ea, Enlil.

There does exist a Babylonian form of the kingship-in-heaven tradition, the *Enuma Elish.*

A similar tradition is, however, also known among other Indo-European peoples.

There is an Iranian form of the tradition (Wikander).

This Persian form is embedded within the account of early Iranian kings found in the *Shāh-nāmeh* ('Book of Kings') by Ferdowsī.

Ferdowsī, or Abū Ol-Qasem Manṣūr, was a Persian poet of the tenth and eleventh centuries AD.

Ferdowsī's poem is based on an earlier Persian tradition.

Given the late date of the *Shāh-nāmeh,* however, the kingship-in-heaven motif may possibly have been borrowed from ancient Near Eastern or Greek sources.

There is a Norse form of the tradition.

The Scandinavian tale is found in the creation account of the *Prose Edda* by Snorri Sturluson.

The work is, again, late, written in the thirteenth century AD, and Snorri had access to Greek traditions.

The possibility that the kingship-in-heaven myth, in each of the forms in which it occurs among Indo-European peoples, was borrowed, rather than inherited from an earlier Indo-European era, cannot be ruled out.

Bibliography and Further Reading

Hoffner, Harry. 1990. *Hittite Myths.* Atlanta: Scholars Press.

Littleton, Scott. 1970. "The 'Kingship in Heaven' Theme." In *Myth and Law Among the Indo-Europeans*, pp. 83–121. Edited by J. Puhvel. Los Angeles: The University of California Press.

Pritchard, J. B. (ed.). 1969. *Ancient Near Eastern Texts Relating to the Old Testament.* 3rd ed. Princeton: Princeton University Press.

Puhvel, Jaan. 1987. "Ancient Greece." In *Comparative Mythology*, pp. 126–143. Baltimore: Johns Hopkins University Press.

West, M. L. 1997. *The East Face of Helicon: West Asiatic Elements in Greek Poetry and Myth*, pp. 276–292. Oxford: Oxford University Press.

_____. 1978. *Hesiod: Theogony.* Reprint edition. Oxford: Clarendon Press.

Wikander, Stig. 1951. "Hethitiska myter hos greker och perser." *Vetenskaps-societeten i Lund*, pp. 35–56.

6 The Gods of Olympus and the Heroes of Ancient Greece

Outline of Key Terms and Concepts

1. Zeus
    - Zeus is the king of gods and mortals.
    - Zeus remains the sky-god, like his Proto-Indo-European ancestor.
        - Zeus is descended from **Dyeus* (see Figure 3.1).
    - Zeus is also characterized by non-Indo-European elements, associated with the island of Crete.
        - Zeus is born in a cave beneath a mountain on Crete.
            - There bees feed Zeus.
            - The goat Amalthea nourishes him.
            - Guards surround him and strike their spears against their shields when he cries so Cronus will not hear him.
        - There was also a Cretan tradition that held that Zeus had died.
        - The Greeks may have acquired these elements from the pre-Greek, Minoan civilization of Crete.
    - The wives of Zeus
        - In his *Theogony* (886–928), Hesiod lists the wives of Zeus.
            - First wife: Metis (an Oceanid)
                - Zeus swallows Metis after Gaea and Uranus warn him of the children she will bear.
                    - She will produce a daughter who will be like him in wisdom and strength.
                    - She will produce a son who will overthrow him as he had overthrown his father, Cronus.
                - Metis is already pregnant with the daughter when Zeus swallows her.
                    - That daughter, Athena, is then born from the head of Zeus.
            - Second wife: Themis (a Titan)
                - The offspring of Zeus and Themis are the Horae ('Seasons') and the Moerae ('Fates').
            - Third wife: Eurynome (an Oceanid)
                - The offspring of Zeus and Eurynome are the Charities or Graces.

They are the embodiment of beauty.

Fourth wife: Demeter

Zeus and Demeter have a daughter, Persephone.

Fifth wife: Mnemosyne ('Memory', a Titan)

The offspring of Zeus and Mnemosyne are the nine Muses, the goddesses of artistic inspiration.

Sixth wife: Leto (daughter of Coeus and Phoebe)

Leto is pregnant by Zeus.

Hera, goddess of childbirth, is jealous of Leto.

Hera decrees that no place on which the sun shines is to allow Leto to give birth.

Poseidon covers the island of Delos with a wave, shading it from the sun.

Leto gives birth to twins, Apollo and Artemis, on Delos.

Seventh wife: Hera

The offspring of Zeus and Hera are:

- Hebe

  Hebe is cupbearer of the gods, waiting upon them as they feast.

  Hebe is the goddess of youth.

  The Romans equate Hebe with Juventas, Roman goddess of young men of military age.

  Hebe will become the wife of the hero Heracles after he ascends to Mt. Olympus.

- Ares
- Eileithyia

  Eileithyia, like her mother Hera, is a goddess of childbirth.

  The Romans identify Eileithyia with Juno Lucina.

- Hephaestus

  Hera is said by some to have conceived Hephaestus on her own (without Zeus).

Dione is also said to be a wife of Zeus, though Hesiod does not present her as such.

Hesiod identifies her as one of the Oceanids.

Dione's name is a feminine form of *Zeus*.

The offspring of Zeus and Dione is Aphrodite, according to some sources.

Exam 1

Zeus and Europa, a mortal "lover"

Europa is the daughter of Agenor.

Agenor is the king of the city of Tyre or Sidon.

Agenor has three sons:

Cadmus

Phoenix: eponymous founder of Phoenicia

Cilix: eponymous founder of Cilicia

Homer (*Iliad* 14.321) identifies Europa's father as Phoenix.

Zeus takes on the form of a bull.

Europa encounters the gentle and playful bull on the shore.

When Europa climbs on the bull's back, he moves out into deep water.

The bull carries Europa through the Mediterranean to Crete.

On Crete, Zeus fathers sons by Europa:

- Minos

  Minos becomes a legendary King of Crete.

  Minos provides the name of the Minoan civilization of Crete.

- Rhadamanthys

  Rhadamanthys is famed for his wisdom.

  Rhadamanthys will become one of the judges of the dead in the realm of Hades.

- Sarpedon

  Sarpedon leaves Crete and settles in Lycia in Anatolia.

  Homer knows a Lycian named Sarpedon, an ally of the Trojans.

Agenor sends Cadmus and his brothers in search of Europa.

Cadmus travels to Greece, where he consults the Delphic oracle of Apollo.

Obeying the instructions he receives there, Cadmus follows a certain cow until it lies down.

At that spot, Cadmus is to found a city.

Cadmus wishes to offer the cow as a sacrifice to Athena.

The companions of Cadmus go to a nearby spring to obtain water for the sacrifice, where they are attacked by a serpent.

The serpent is said to be a son of the god Ares.

Cadmus hears the sounds of combat, rushes to the spring, and kills the serpent.

Following the instructions of Athena, Cadmus removes the teeth of the serpent and sows them in the ground.

From the sown teeth, armed warriors, the Spartoi, spring up out of the ground.

The Spartoi fight and kill one another; five survive.

At the site, Cadmus establishes the Greek city of Thebes.

For slaying the serpent, offspring of Ares, Cadmus must serve Ares as a slave for a period of time.

When his servitude has ended, Cadmus becomes king of Thebes and marries Harmonia, a daughter of Ares and Aphrodite.

2. Hera

Hera is one of the daughters of Cronus and Rhea.

Hera is principal wife of Zeus.

Hera is goddess of women, marriage, and childbirth.

3. Poseidon

Poseidon is one of the sons of Cronus and Rhea.

Poseidon is god of the sea.

The Greeks have other sea-gods:

- Nereus: an Old Man of the Sea

  Nereus is a son of Gaea and Pontus.

  Nereus is a shape-shifter.

  Doris (an Oceanid) is the wife of Nereus.

  The offspring of Doris and Nereus are the Nereids, fifty (or more) mermaid-like sea-deities.

- Proteus: another Old Man of the Sea

  Proteus is a seal herder.

  Proteus is a shape-shifter.

  Proteus possesses all knowledge.

Poseidon is god of earthquakes.

One of his epithets is "Earth-Shaker."

Poseidon is god of horses.

An Arcadian tradition of Poseidon and Demeter:

Demeter Erinys takes on horse-form.

Poseidon does the same and mates with her.

Demeter gives birth to two offspring:

A son: the horse, Areion

A daughter: sometimes called Despoina (mistress of the netherworld)

4. Demeter

Demeter is one of the daughters of Cronus and Rhea.

Demeter is goddess of grain and agriculture.

Demeter is mother of Persephone (fathered by Zeus).

Hades abducts Persephone.

The scene of the abduction is variously given.

The Meadows of Enna in Sicily is a common locale.

Hades carries Persephone to the netherworld in his chariot.

Demeter searches for Persephone.

Demeter lights torches from the flames of volcanic Mt. Etna and searches the earth.

Helios tells Demeter of the abduction.

Demeter grieves and earth does not produce vegetation.

Zeus tells Hades to release Persephone.

Persephone eats a pomegranate seed while she is in the netherworld.

As a consequence, Persephone must spend a portion of each year in the netherworld.

One-third of the year Persephone lives with Hades.

Two-thirds of the year Persephone lives with Demeter.

5. Hades

Hades is god of the netherworld.

Hades' name may be of Indo-European origin.

His name is possibly derived from the Proto-Indo-European root **weid-* 'to see'.

Hades would then mean 'unseen'.

The Romans identify Hades with their god Dis Pater.

Latin *Dis* 'rich one' is a translation of Greek *Pluto*, another name used for Hades.

Homer (*Iliad* 15.187–193) describes how Zeus and his two brothers had divided up the cosmos by casting lots.

Zeus receives sovereignty over earth.

Poseidon receives sovereignty over sea.

Hades receives sovereignty over the underworld.

The Greeks probably borrowed this tradition from the Near East (Burkert).

A similar tale is told in the Babylonian *Atrahasis*, a creation and flood account.

6. Hephaestus

Hephaestus is a god of fire and arts.

Hephaestus is the smith of the gods.

Hephaestus was once thrown out of heaven.

According to one tradition, Hera throws Hephaestus out of heaven (Homer, *Iliad* 18.394–409).

This was a consequence of his physical deformity: Hephaestus is lame.

Hephaestus is rescued by Thetis (a Nereid) and Eurynome (an Oceanid).

According to another tradition, Zeus throws Hephaestus out of heaven (Homer, *Iliad* 1.571–594).

This was a consequence of Hephaestus meddling in a quarrel between Zeus and Hera.

Hephaestus lands on Lemnos, where he is rescued by a people of that island.

One of the extraordinary implements that Hephaestus crafts is the shield of Achilles (Homer, *Iliad* 18.368–617).

The Greeks are at war with Troy.

Achilles, the greatest of the Greek heroes at Troy, refuses to fight.

Patroclus, the close friend of Achilles, goes into battle wearing Achilles' armor.

Patroclus is slain and Achilles' armor is lost.

Thetis, the mother of Achilles, asks Hephaestus to craft new armor for her son.

The shield that Hephaestus makes for Achilles is a work of art on which are depicted several scenes.

The physical world is depicted:

- Earth, sky, sea
- Sun, moon, stars
- Ocean streams around the edge

There is a scene of a city at peace:

- Wedding festivals in progress
- A panel of judges deciding a case

There is a scene of a city at war:

- A city under siege
- Cattle and flocks being stolen
- A battle being waged

There is a scene of agrarian activities:

- The ploughing of farmlands
- The harvesting of grain and grapes
- The herding of cattle and the pasturing of sheep

Homer's account of the shield of Achilles appears to preserve a Greek expression of the ancestral Indo-European tripartite ideology (Yoshida).

First function (the city at peace):

- Religious aspect: marriage rites
- Legal aspect: judgment

Second function (the city at war): scenes of war making

Third function: scenes of agricultural activity

7. Ares
   - Ares is the god of war and carnage.
   - Ares is well-known for his affair with Aphrodite.
     - Aphrodite is the wife of Hephaestus.
     - Helios tells Hephaestus of the affair.
     - Hephaestus crafts a net, delicate but strong.
     - Hephaestus places the net over Aphrodite's bed and traps the lovers.
     - Hephaestus calls in the gods to witness the spectacle.
   - Ares has a daughter Alcippe, whose mother is Aglaurus of Athens.
     - Halirrhothius, a son of Poseidon, tries to rape Alcippe.
     - Ares kills Halirrhothius.
       - A panel of gods judges Ares on a hill in Athens.
         - The place is then known as the Hill of Ares, or the Areopagus.
         - Historically, the Areopagus was the meeting place of the Athenian council.
       - Ares is sentenced to be a slave to a mortal man for one year.
8. Aphrodite
   - Aphrodite is the goddess of love.
   - Among her many romances, one that is well known is her affair with Adonis.
     - There was a king of Cyprus named Cinyras.
     - Cinyras has a daughter, Myrrha.
     - Myrrha has an incestuous desire for her father.
     - Myrrha's desire is satisfied with the assistance of her old nurse.
     - Myrrha flees from her father when he, horrified, discovers the identity of his new lover (at first hidden by darkness).
     - Myrrha wanders as a fugitive, carrying her father's child within her womb.
     - Before the child is born, Myrrha calls upon the gods for help.
       - Myrrha wishes neither to live nor to die.
     - The gods transform Myrrha into a tree (the myrrh tree).
     - From this tree, the baby Adonis is born.
     - There are two traditions about how Aphrodite meets Adonis.
       - Aphrodite encounters Adonis: tradition 1 (Apollodorus 3.14.4).
         - Aphrodite discovers the baby Adonis.
         - Aphrodite entrusts him to Persephone as a caregiver.
         - Both Aphrodite and Persephone then want Adonis.
         - Zeus passes judgment:
           - One-third of the year Adonis is to live with Persephone in the netherworld.

- One-third of the year Adonis is to live with Aphrodite.
- One-third of the year Adonis is to live with whom he chooses.

Adonis chooses Aphrodite.

Aphrodite encounters Adonis: tradition 2 (Ovid, *Metamorphoses* 10.503–532).

The Naiads (nymphs of springs) discover the baby Adonis.

Adonis grows to be a young man.

One day, Cupid accidentally grazes Aphrodite with one of his arrows.

As a consequence, when Aphrodite sees Adonis, soon afterward, she falls in love with him.

Though Aphrodite warns her new lover, Adonis, not to go hunting, he does so anyway.

Adonis is fatally wounded by a wild boar.

Ares either sent the boar, or Ares was the boar.

Aphrodite finds the dying Adonis.

In her grief, Aphrodite creates a flower from his blood as a memorial.

9. Athena

Athena is the virgin warrior goddess and patron deity of Athens.

Zeus and Metis are Athena's parents.

Athena was "delivered" by Hephaestus from the head of Zeus after he swallowed Metis.

Athena is beautiful, as is told in the tale of "The Judgment of Paris."

The story begins at the marriage feast of Peleus and Thetis.

Eris (goddess of envy) throws an apple onto the table.

On the apple is written: "For the most beautiful."

Hera, Athena, and Aphrodite each lay claim to the apple.

Paris, a Trojan prince, is chosen to judge which goddess is the most beautiful of the three.

Hermes conducts the three goddesses to Paris.

Each goddess offers Paris a bribe:

- Hera, wife of the king of gods, offers sovereignty.
- Athena, warrior goddess, offers victory in battle.
- Aphrodite, goddess of love, offers Helen, the most beautiful of mortal women.

Paris judges Aphrodite to be the most beautiful.

Aphrodite will assist Paris in abducting Helen.

Helen is the wife of Menelaus, the king of Sparta.

Events are thereby set in motion that will culminate in the Trojan War.

The Greeks will send a vast fleet of ships and warriors against Troy to recover Helen.

The bribes offered by the goddesses in the Greek tradition of "The Judgment of Paris" preserve the archaic Indo-European tripartite ideology (Dumézil 1995:608–614):

- First function: the promise of sovereignty
- Second function: the promise of success in war making
- Third function: the promise of sensual fulfillment

Athena is also goddess of crafts and arts.

Athena is the inventor of the *aulos*.

The *aulos* is a wind instrument—a pipe (usually double) fitted with a reed and drilled with finger-holes.

Athena discards the *aulos* out of vanity, concerned that playing it is distorting her face.

Marsyas discovers the discarded *aulos*.

Marsyas is a satyr.

Satyrs are male demigods of the wild.

Satyrs are portrayed as partially human-like, partially beast-like, with features such as a horse's tail and a goat's legs, ears, horns.

Satyrs form a part of the retinue of Dionysus.

Silenus is the chief of the satyrs.

Silenus is depicted as a fat, jolly old man, often drunk.

Riding on an ass, Silenus accompanies Dionysus.

According to some, Silenus raised Dionysus.

Marsyas challenges Apollo to a musical contest.

Apollo accepts, on the condition that the winner can do whatever he would like to the loser.

Apollo plays the lyre.

The judges of the contest are variously identified: Muses; Midas (king of Phrygia).

Marsyas and Apollo are equally good.

Apollo wins by playing his lyre upside down, a feat that Marsyas cannot match with his wind instrument.

When Apollo is judged the winner, he flays Marsyas.

Athena is also a weaver and spinner.

Arachne, a girl of Lydia who is an accomplished weaver, boasts that her skills rival Athena's.

Athena appears to Arachne disguised as an old woman and tries to persuade her to put an end to her boasting.

Arachne is unmoved and challenges Athena to a weaving contest.

Athena weaves a beautiful tapestry of the Olympian deities in their glory.

Arachne weaves a beautiful tapestry of the Olympian deities engaged in debauchery.

Both Athena and Arachne produce magnificent tapestries.

Athena destroys Arachne's tapestry and beats her with a shuttle.

Arachne tries to hang herself.

Athena turns Arachne into a spider.

10. Hermes

Hermes is a god of numerous functions.

Hermes is the god of roads and journeys.

Columns depicting the god and called "Herms" were commonly placed at crossroads in Greece.

Hermes is a psychopomp, conducting the souls of the dead to Hades.

Hermes is god of flocks and herds, and he protects herders.

Hermes is god of wealth, merchants, and thieves.

Hermes is a messenger god.

Hermes is the son of Zeus and Maia, daughter of Atlas.

The *Homeric Hymn to Hermes* rehearses the events that follow his birth in Maia's cave in Arcadia's Mt. Cyllene.

Soon after birth, Hermes leaves the cave and finds a tortoise.

Hermes crafts a lyre from the tortoise's shell and composes songs.

Hermes then travels up to the north of Greece, to Pieria (close to Mt. Olympus).

Hermes there drives off 50 cows from Apollo's herd of cattle.

Hermes turns the hooves of the cattle in different directions, and he himself walks backward to confuse anyone who might try to track them.

Hermes then makes wicker sandals for his feet.

An old man sees him driving the cattle; Hermes instructs him to tell no one.

The cattle drive continues, and as dawn approaches, Hermes sacrifices two of the cattle.

Hermes returns home to Maia's cave and slips into his cradle.

Apollo discovers the theft.

The old man reports to Apollo what he had seen and the identity of the thief.

Apollo confronts Hermes in Maia's cave.

Hermes tells Apollo to let Zeus judge between them.

Zeus, judge of the Olympians, directs Hermes to show Apollo where his cattle are.

Hermes does so and compensates Apollo with the lyre he had made.

Apollo asks Zeus to confer on Hermes the various attributes for which he is known.

Hermes and Aphrodite produce a son, Hermaphroditus.

Naiads, nymphs of springs, raise Hermaphroditus.

When Hermaphroditus becomes a young man, he leaves home and travels about Lycia and Caria.

In his travels, Hermaphroditus one day comes upon the pool of Salmacis, a nymph.

Salmacis openly expresses her desire for Hermaphroditus, but he reproaches her.

Thinking Salmacis has gone, Hermaphroditus disrobes and dives into the pool.

Salmacis, watching, then swims to Hermaphroditus and embraces him.

Hermaphroditus struggles to break free; Salmacis struggles to hold on.

Salmacis prays that the gods will never let them be separated.

The bodies of Hermaphroditus and Salmacis are fused into one.

11. Apollo

Apollo is a god of healing.

His common epithet is *Paean* 'healer'.

In the Linear B texts of the Mycenaeans, *Paean* may denote Apollo.

Apollo is also a warrior god, whose weapon is a silver bow.

Homer begins his *Iliad* with an incident in which the warrior Apollo figures prominently.

It is the tenth year of the Trojan War.

The Greek warriors have abducted a young woman named Chryseis.

Chryseis is the daughter of Apollo's priest, Chryses.

Agamemnon, leader of the Greeks who have sailed to war against Troy, refuses to hand over Chryseis to her father, who has come to beg for her return.

Agamemnon threatens the old priest Chryses and sends him away without his daughter.

Chryses prays that Apollo Smintheus will punish the Greeks.

Smintheus is a title of Apollo.

Smintheus appears to be derived from Greek *smínthos* 'mouse'.

Strabo, the Greek geographer (first centuries BC and AD) writes of a temple of Apollo Smintheus in Chrysa in the Troad (Strabo 13.1.48).

At the temple, there is an image of Apollo with his foot upon a mouse.

Answering the prayer of Chryses, Apollo shoots his arrows into the Greeks and their animals.

A plague comes upon them.

An Indo-European deity with similar characteristics, Rudra, is found in ancient India (Puhvel; Grégoire; Dumézil 1987).

Rudra is a warrior god whose weapon is the bow (*Rig Veda* 2.33.14).

Rudra is a healing god (*Rig Veda* 2.33.2, 4).

Apollo has a son, Asclepius.

Asclepius is the son of Apollo and Coronis.

Coronis is the daughter of Phlegyas, a king of the Lapiths.

The Lapiths are identified as a people of Thessaly, in the north of Greece.

The Lapiths also appear in Greek mythic tradition as the opponents of the Centaurs.

Coronis, pregnant with Asclepius, is unfaithful to Apollo and he consequently kills her.

Apollo removes Asclepius from her womb.

Apollo hands Asclepius over to the Centaur Chiron, who trains Asclepius in the healing arts.

Asclepius is famed as a great healer.

The cult of Asclepius the healer had its center at Epidaurus.

The name *Asclepius*, like *Smintheus*, may be derived from a Greek word for a rodent (Grégoire).

Aspálaks occurs beside *spálaks* as the name of a type of mole.

Skálops (with *k* and *p* reversed) is a third and older variant.

That *skálops* is the older form is revealed by cognates, such as Latin *scalpo* 'I scratch'.

Some scholars conjecture that an additional variant, **askálops*, must have also occurred.

**Askálops* is then a possible source of the name *Asclepius*.

Supporting evidence is said to be provided by the architecture of the temple of Asclepius at Epidaurus.

An associated structure at the temple, a *tholos*, appears to have been constructed to suggest a mole's den.

In India, Rudra has a son, Gaṇeśa.

Gaṇeśa is affiliated with the rat.

Rudra is affiliated with the mole.

Greek Apollo and Asclepius and Indic Rudra and Gaṇeśa may be a homologous pair.

The Greek and Indic pair would be descended from a common Proto-Indo-European duo having the following configuration:

- A warrior god who slays with the bow, but who also heals.
- The god is associated with a rodent.
- The god has a son with similar characteristics.

12. Artemis

Artemis is a virgin goddess of the hunt.

Artemis is a goddess of childbirth.

Artemis shares this role with Hera and Eileithyia.

Ephesian Artemis appears to be depicted as a Mother Goddess.

A tale is told of Artemis and her encounter with Actaeon, as by Ovid (*Metamorphoses* 3.138–252).

Actaeon is a grandson of Cadmus.

While hunting one day, Actaeon wanders into a grove sacred to Artemis.

Within a stream within a cave in this grove, Actaeon sees Artemis bathing.

Artemis throws water onto Acteon's head.

Acteon is transformed into a deer as the water runs down his body.

Actaeon runs from the cave and is chased and killed by his own hounds.

Alternative traditions are attested.

Actaeon dies for boasting that he is a better hunter than Artemis (Euripides, *Bacchae* 337–340).

Actaeon dies for proposing to Artemis (Diodorus Siculus 4.81.4).

Zeus kills Acteon because of the young man's love interests in Semele (Acusilaus, fragment 33).

Ovid also knows the tale of Artemis and Callisto (*Metamorphoses* 2.409–507; *Fasti* 2.153–192).

Callisto is Artemis's favorite nymph attendant.

Greek *númphe* 'nymph' has several meanings:

'Woman of marriageable age'; 'bride'; 'married woman.'

The nymphs of Greek myth are female personifications of nature.

Several distinct types of nymphs can be identified:

- Oceanids

  The Oceanids are the 3,000 daughters of the Titans Oceanus and Tethys.

  Metis and Eurynome are Oceanids.

- Naiads

  The Naiads are nymphs of flowing waters.

  Naiads found Adonis and raised Hermaphroditus.

- Leimoniads

  The Leimoniads are nymphs of meadows.

- Oreads

  The Oreads are nymphs of mountains.

- Meliae

  The Meliae are daughters of Gaea and Uranus, conceived at the castration of Uranus.

  The Meliae are nymphs of ash trees.

- Dryads; Hamadryads

  Callisto and other of the attendants of Artemis are Dryads.

  The Dryads are nymphs of trees.

  The name *Dryad* comes from Greek *drûs* 'tree, oak'.

  Greek *drûs* is from the Proto-Indo-European root **deru-* 'tree'.

  Celtic *Druid* may be derived from the same root.

  A Dryad is also called a *Hamadryad* (from Greek *hama-* 'at the same time with') because she lives only as long as the tree in which she dwells.

Zeus encounters Callisto in Arcadia.

Zeus disguises himself as Artemis to catch Callisto off guard.

Zeus rapes Callisto.

Artemis discovers Callisto's pregnancy on a warm day when the nymphs disrobe for a swim.

Artemis banishes Callisto from her presence.

Callisto gives birth to a son, Arcas.

- *Arcas* is the eponym of Arcadia.
- The name *Arcas* is similar to the Greek word for 'bear', *árktos*.

Hera, the jealous wife of Zeus, transforms Callisto into a bear.

Arcas encounters this bear when he has grown to be a young man.

Before he can kill the bear, Zeus transforms mother and son into constellations.

- Callisto (the bear) becomes Ursa Major (the 'Great Bear').
- Arcas becomes Arctophylax (the 'Bear Guardian').

13. Dionysus

Dionysus is the god of wine and revelry.

Dionysus is also called Bacchus.

- The name *Bacchus* may be borrowed from Lydian *Baki-*.

Dionysus is the son of Zeus and Semele (Apollodorus 3.4.3).

- In Greek tradition, Semele is presented as a daughter of Cadmus.
  - Greek Semele is probably ultimately related to Indo-European earth-goddesses such as Slavic Mati Syra Zemlja, Latvian Zemes Mate.
  - The Greek name Semele is borrowed from another Indo-European language, probably Thracian, rather than being inherited.
    - Thracian is a so-called "minor" Indo-European language (not belonging to any of the ten major Indo-European subfamilies).
      - Some scholars have claimed that Thracian is closely related to another minor Indo-European language, Phrygian.
        - Phrygian was spoken in Anatolia after the demise of the Hittites.
- Semele is one of Zeus's lovers.
- Hera disguises herself as Semele's old nursemaid.
- Hera persuades Semele to ask Zeus to come to her in all of his glory.
- Zeus consents and Semele is consumed by fire.
- Zeus rescues the unborn Dionysus from Semele's ashes.
- Zeus sews the fetus into his own leg, from which Dionysus is born.

Scholars once thought Dionysus came late to the Greek pantheon.

- Dionysus appears, however, in the Linear B tablets; hence, he is not later than the second-millennium BC Mycenaean Greek civilization.
- The worship of Dionysus was probably introduced into Greece from Thrace.

- Young Dionysus
  - Ino, sister of Semele, is caregiver for Dionysus (Ovid, *Metamorphoses* 4.416–562).
    - Jealous Hera drives Ino and her husband, Athamas, mad.
    - Athamas kills their son Learchus.
    - Ino jumps from a cliff into the sea with their son Melicertes.
    - Poseidon transforms Ino and Melicertes into sea deities.
      - Ino becomes Leucothea.
      - Melicertes becomes Palaemon.
  - The nymphs of Mt. Nysa raise Dionysus.
    - The location of Mt. Nysa is unknown.
      - *Nysa* may be related to the second portion of the name of the god, Dio-*nysus*.
    - These nymphs remain perpetually young (Ovid, *Metamorphoses* 7.262–296).
      - Their perpetual youth is provided by a potion concocted by the enchantress Medea.
- The worship of Dionysus
  - Worship of Dionysus was characterized by ecstasy and crazed brutality.
  - Many of his devotees appear to have been women.
  - Worshippers would sacrifice animals by tearing the creature apart.
    - Omophagy, consumption of the victim's raw flesh, was practiced.
  - Worshippers typically carried a *thyrsus:* an ivy-covered rod.
- Dionysus and Lycurgus (Homer, *Iliad* 6:130–144)
  - Lycurgus is a king of Thrace.
  - Lycurgus attacks Dionysus and his nymphs.
    - Some of the nymphs are killed.
    - Dionysus escapes by diving into the sea.
  - Lycurgus is blinded by Zeus and goes mad.
  - Lycurgus dies hated by all the gods.
- Dionysus and Pentheus (Ovid, *Metamorphoses* 3.511–733)
  - Pentheus is a grandson of Cadmus and the king of Thebes.
  - Pentheus opposes the worship of Dionysus.
  - Pentheus goes to Mt. Cithaeron to observe the followers of Dionysus as they worship the god.
  - Agave, his own mother, and other worshippers attack and kill Pentheus.
- Dionysus and the daughters of Proetus, the Proetides (Apollodorus 2.2.2)

Proetus is king in Tiryns.

The Proetides refuse to worship Dionysus.

Dionysus drives the Proetides mad.

Melampus offers to cure them.

Melampus is a famous prophet.

As a child, he gave certain dead snakes a proper funeral.

The snakes' offspring purified the ears of Melampus as he slept.

Melampus thereby learned the speech of birds.

Melampus cures the Proetides and receives part of their father's kingdom in return.

14. Heracles

Heracles is the son of Zeus and Alcmena (Apollodorus 2.4.8–10; Diodorus Siculus 4.9.1–10.1).

Alcmena is the daughter of Electryon (king of Mycenae) and the wife of Amphitryon.

Zeus determines to engender a son by Alcmena.

In Amphitryon's absence, Zeus comes to Alcmena in the disguise of her husband for a period equivalent to three nights.

Alcmena conceives a child by Zeus: Heracles.

Alcmena immediately thereafter conceives a child by Amphitryon: Iphicles.

On the day when Heracles is to be born, Zeus announces in the presence of the gods that the child born that day would be king of the Argives.

Hera, with the assistance of Eileithyia, slows the labor of Alcmena.

Eurystheus, a cousin of Heracles, is instead born that day.

Zeus and Hera reach a compromise:

Eurystheus will become king.

Heracles will serve him, performing any twelve labors that Eurystheus chooses.

Afterward, Heracles will be given immortality.

Following his birth, Hera sends two snakes to kill baby Heracles.

Heracles strangles the snakes.

Heracles: the "triple-sinning warrior"

Dumézil (1983; 1970) has identified the recurring motif of an Indo-European warrior who commits a sin against each of the three functions.

The triple-sinning warrior is widely distributed across Indo-European cultures and must be descended from such a figure in the parent Indo-European mythic tradition.

Heracles' first-function sin: The failure to obey Zeus (Diodorus Siculus 4.10.6–11.1)

- Zeus commands Heracles to serve Eurystheus, his cousin and king in Argos.
- Heracles visits the Delphic oracle to learn what he should do.
- The oracle instructs Heracles to serve Eurystheus and perform twelve labors.
- Heracles despairs at the command.
- Hera sends a fit of madness on Heracles and he murders his children.
- Heracles becomes slave to Eurystheus.
- The Twelve Labors of Heracles (Apollodorus 2.5.1–12)
  - First labor: The Nemean Lion
    - The Nemean lion is an invincible offspring of Typhoeus that was raised by Hera.
      - For Hesiod (*Theogony* 327), the lion is the offspring of Orthus, who is in turn an offspring of Typhoeus and Echidna (see below).
    - Heracles strangles the lion.
    - Heracles removes its pelt (for his cape), using the lion's own claws.
  - Second labor: The Lernaean Hydra
    - The Hydra is a nine-headed swamp serpent.
    - The Hydra is offspring of Typhoeus and Echidna.
      - Echidna is a monstrous creature, part woman, part snake.
      - According to Hesiod (*Theogony* 297), Echidna is the offspring of Phorcys and Ceto, who are themselves the offspring of Pontus and Gaea.
    - The Hydra is assisted by a great crab.
    - Heracles is assisted by Iolaus, his nephew.
    - Heracles begins cutting off each of the Hydra's heads.
    - As Heracles does so, two heads grow back in the place of one.
    - Iolaus cauterizes the stump of each decapitated neck so that new heads cannot grow.
    - Heracles poisons his arrows by dipping the point of each in the Hydra's blood.
  - Third labor: The Cerynitian Hind

- The Cerynitian Hind is a deer with golden antlers, sacred to Artemis.
- Heracles chases the deer for one year.
- Artemis and Apollo confront Heracles after he has caught it.
- Heracles persuades the gods to let him return to Eursytheus with the deer.

Fourth labor: The Erymanthian Boar

- This is a great boar of Mt. Erymanthus.
- Heracles chases the boar into a snow bank.
- Heracles captures the boar with a noose.
- Heracles carries the boar to Eurystheus.

Fifth labor: The Augean Stables

- Augeas, a son of Helios, owns many cattle.
- Eurystheus orders Heracles to clean out the stables of Augeas.
- Heracles tells Augeas he will clean the stables in a single day in return for one-tenth of his cattle.
- Heracles diverts two rivers to flow through the stable lots and cleans them out.
- Augeas, however, refuses to pay Heracles.
- Heracles will eventually kill Augeas.

Sixth labor: The Stymphalian Birds

- A great flock of birds is roosting in the trees around Lake Stymphalis.
- Athena gives Heracles bronze rattles with which to scare the birds.
- Heracles shoots the frightened birds as they fly away.

Seventh labor: The Cretan Bull

- This creature is a wild bull of Crete.
- There are variant traditions about its origin.
  - According to some, it is the bull that carried Europa for Zeus.
  - According to others, it is a bull that Poseidon sent to Minos, king of Crete.
- Heracles captures the bull and returns with it to Eurystheus.
- Eurystheus releases the bull.
  - The bull wanders to Marathon.
  - Theseus later kills the bull.

Eighth labor: The Horses of Diomedes

- Diomedes is a son of Ares and a king in Thrace.

- Diomedes owns flesh-eating horses.
- Heracles kills Diomedes and feeds his flesh to the horses.
- Heracles corrals the horses and delivers them to Eurystheus.

Ninth labor: The Amazon's Girdle

- Hippolyta is the queen of the Amazons, a race of women warriors.
- Hippolyta owns the belt (girdle) of Ares.
- Admete, daughter of Eurystheus, desires the belt.
- Heracles sails to the city of the Amazons and meets with Hippolyta.
- Hera, disguised as an Amazon, rouses the Amazons.
- The Amazons attack Heracles.
- Heracles kills Hippolyta.
- Heracles delivers the belt to Eurystheus.

Tenth labor: The Cattle of Geryon

- Geryon is a three-bodied man, owning red cattle pastured on the distant island of Erythea.
- Eurytion is his giant herdsman.
- Orthus is a two-headed dog, offspring of Echidna and Typhoeus, that guards the cattle.
- Heracles travels across the ocean in the golden cup of Helios.
- Heracles slays Orthus, Eurytion, and Geryon.
- Heracles sails back with the cattle in the cup and drives them across Europe to Eurystheus.
- Eurystheus sacrifices the cattle to Hera.

Eleventh labor: The Apples of the Hesperides

- The Hesperides are the daughters of Night, who have a garden in the far west.
- In this garden grows a tree with golden apples.
- Ladon is a hundred-headed dragon that guards the tree; it is the offspring of Echidna and Typhoeus.
    - Heracles kills Ladon.
- Heracles holds up heaven for Atlas.
- Atlas picks the apples for Heracles.
- Heracles tricks Atlas into taking back the burden of heaven.
- Heracles delivers the apples to Eurystheus.
- Athena returns the apples to the garden.

- Twelfth labor: The Capture of Cerberus
  - Cerberus is the three-headed dog of Hades.
  - Cerberus is another offspring of Echidna and Typhoeus.
  - After descending to Hades, Heracles encounters the shades of Meleager, Medusa, and others.
  - Heracles overpowers Cerberus and delivers him to Eurystheus.
  - Eurystheus wants Cerberus returned to Hades and Heracles takes him back.
  - There is a Homeric variant (*Iliad* 5.395–397) of this account in which Heracles wounds Hades.

Heracles' second-function sin: The cowardly murder of a fellow warrior (Diodorus Siculus 4.31.1–4).

- Eurytus is the king of Oechalia.
- Iole is the daughter of the king.
- Eurytus holds an archery contest to find a husband for Iole.
- Heracles wins the contest but is denied the prize.
- Iphitus is the brother of Iole.
- Iphitus visits Heracles in Tiryns, searching for some missing cattle.
- Heracles hurls unsuspecting Iphitus from a tower.
- As a consequence, disease comes upon Heracles.
- Heracles visits the Delphic oracle to find out how to be healed.
- Heracles is told he must sell himself into slavery.
- Omphale, the queen of Lydia, purchases Heracles.
- Heracles serves Omphale in women's clothing (Ovid, *Fasti* 2.305–358).
  - Heracles here plays the part of the Indo-European cross-dressing warrior (Puhvel 1987).
    - Such a warrior figure is found in several Indo-European traditions.
  - In Greece there is a second such figure: Achilles.
    - Chiron, the Centaur, is the teacher of Achilles.
    - The Greek seer Calchas prophesies that the Greeks cannot capture Troy without Achilles.
    - Thetis, the mother of Achilles, does not want Achilles to go to war.
    - Thetis takes Achilles out of Chiron's care.
    - Thetis sends Achilles to live with the daughters of King Lycomedes of Scyros.
    - Achilles dresses himself as a girl.

- Odysseus and Diomedes, two of the leading Greek warriors preparing to go to war with Troy, search for Achilles.
- Their searching takes them to Scyros.
- Odysseus and Diomedes show weapons to the girls and cause a war trumpet to be blown.
- One of the "girls" reaches for the weapons.
- Achilles is discovered.

Heracles completes his servitude to Omphale and is released.

Heracles' third-function sin: abduction of women (Diodorus Siculus 4.37.4–38.5)

Heracles had encountered the shade of Meleager in Hades when he went to capture Cerberus for Eurystheus.

- Meleager was son of King Oeneus of Calydon.
- Soon after the birth of Meleager, the Moerae, or Fates, appeared to his mother, Althaea.
    - The Fates are daughters of Zeus and Themis.
    - The Fates are three hags who determine the destiny of humans.
        - Clotho spins the thread of life.
        - Lachesis measures the thread.
        - Atropus cuts the thread.
- The Fates foretell that the babe, Meleager, will die as soon as the log which then burns on the hearth is consumed by fire.
- Althaea removes the log from the hearth, extinguishes the fire, and hides the log away.
- The Calydonian Boar Hunt (Apollodorus 1.8.2–3)
    - Meleager has grown to be a man.
    - Artemis sends a great destructive boar to Calydon.
        - Oeneus, Meleager's father, has mistakenly neglected to include Artemis in the harvest offerings.
    - Oeneus organizes a hunting party, consisting of many heroes, including the woman Atalanta.
    - Atalanta is the first to shoot the boar.
    - Meleager kills the boar with his spear.
    - Meleager chooses to give the prize of the boar's pelt to Atalanta.
    - Meleager's uncles object and Meleager kills them.

        - When Althaea learns of the death of her brothers, angry, she throws the fated log into the fire.
        - Meleager dies.
- In the netherworld, the shade of Meleager asks Heracles to marry his sister, Deianira.
- Heracles wrestles Achelous for Deianira (Apollodorus 2.7.5–6).
    - Achelous is a river god.
    - Achelous takes on the form of a bull to fight Heracles.
    - Heracles defeats Achelous, breaking off one of the bull's horns.
    - Heracles returns the horn to Achelous and receives in its place the cornucopia.
        - The cornucopia is one of the horns of Amalthea.
        - The cornucopia perpetually refills itself with food and drink.
- Heracles marries Deianira in Calydon.
- Heracles and Deianira leave Calydon for Trachis.
    - On the way, they come to a stream where Nessus, a Centaur, offers to take Deianira across.
    - Nessus attempts to rape Deianira.
    - Heracles shoots Nessus with one of his poisoned arrows.
    - The dying Nessus tells Deianira to save some of his blood and semen as a love potion in case Heracles' love for her should diminish.
- Heracles and Astydamia
    - Astydamia is daughter of Ormenius, king of Pelasgiotis.
    - Heracles asks Ormenius for his daughter as a wife.
    - Ormenius refuses because Heracles has a wife.
    - Heracles kills Ormenius and abducts Astydamia.
    - Astydamia conceives a son, Ctesippus, by Heracles.
- Heracles and Iole
    - Angry at being denied Iole, Heracles now attacks and kills the remaining brothers of Iole.
    - Heracles abducts Iole.
    - Heracles wishes to offer a sacrifice to Zeus.
    - Heracles sends Lichas, his herald, to bring his sacrificial robe from Deianira.
    - Deianira pours the Centaur's love potion on the robe.
    - Heracles dons the robe and approaches the sacrificial flame.

            - The heat of the flame activates the poison in the potion.
            - The robe clings to Heracles and the poison seeps into his body.
            - Heracles inquires of the Delphic oracle what can be done to end his suffering.
            - The oracle directs Heracles to prepare a funeral pyre on Mt. Oeta.
            - Philoctetes agrees to light the pyre in exchange for Heracles' bow and arrows.
            - As his body burns, the immortal portion of Heracles ascends to Mt. Olympus.
            - Heracles marries Hebe, daughter of Hera and Zeus.

- Agamemnon: a "triple-sinning warrior"? (Evans)
    - The Greeks have gathered at Aulis to sail to Troy.
    - Favorable winds will not blow.
        - Artemis withholds the winds.
        - Agamemnon had killed her sacred deer.
        - Artemis demands the sacrifice of Iphigenia, daughter of Agamemnon and Clytemnestra.
    - Agamemnon's first-function sin: the sacrifice of his daughter Iphigenia (a sacrilege; Aeschylus, *Agamemnon* 40–257).
    - Favorable winds then blow and the Greeks sail to Troy.
    - Troy falls to the Greeks after many years of war.
    - Agamemnon's second-function sin: the great slaughter of Greek warrior life to rescue his brother's unfaithful wife (Aeschylus, *Agamemnon* 355–488).
    - Agamemnon's third-function sin: associated with the adultery of Helen and greed for wealth (Aeschylus, *Agamemnon* 681–809).
    - Agamemnon's role as triple-sinning warrior is further evidenced by his "three-fold death."
        - Agamemnon returns home to Clytemnestra after the war.
        - Clytemnestra murders Agamemnon (Aeschylus, *Agamemnon* and *Choephoroi*).
        - Agamemnon's death has been interpreted as a triple atonement.
            - Third-function atonement: while Agamemnon is bathing, Clytemnestra entangles him in his robe, like a catch of fish taken in a net.
            - Second-function atonement: Clytemnestra stabs Agamemnon with his weapon—three times.
            - First-function atonement: Aeschylus denotes the tub in which Agamemnon dies using a Greek word for a priestly vessel that holds holy water (*lébēs*).

Bibliography and Further Reading

Brixhe, Claude. 2004. "Phrygian." In Roger Woodard, *The Cambridge Encyclopedia of the World's Ancient Languages*, pp. 777–788. Cambridge: Cambridge University Press.

Burkert, Walter. 1992. *The Orientalizing Revolution*. Cambridge: Harvard University Press.

Dumézil, Georges. 1995. *Mythe et épopée I. II. III.* Paris: Gallimard.

_____. 1987. *Apollon Sonore*. Paris: Gallimard.

_____. 1983. *The Stakes of the Warrior*. Berkeley and Los Angeles: The University of California Press.

_____. 1970. *The Destiny of the Warrior*. Chicago: University of Chicago Press.

Evans, David. 1979. "Agamemnon and the Indo-European Three-fold Death Pattern." *History of Religions* 19:153–166.

Graf, Fritz. 1993. *Greek Mythology*. Baltimore. Johns Hopkins University Press.

Grégoire, H. 1949. *Asclèpios, Apollon Smintheus et Rudra*. Bruxelles: Palais des Académies.

Grimal, Pierre. 1997. *The Dictionary of Classical Mythology*. Oxford: Blackwell.

Mallory, J. P., and D. Q. Adams. 1997. *Encyclopedia of Indo-European Culture*. London and Chicago: Fitzroy Dearborn Publishers.

Newman, Harold, and Jon Newman. 2003. *A Genealogical Chart of Greek Mythology*. Chapel Hill: University of North Carolina Press.

Puhvel, Jaan. 1987. "Ancient Greece." In *Comparative Mythology*, pp. 126–143. Baltimore: Johns Hopkins University Press.

_____. 1970. "Mythological Reflections of Indo-European Medicine." In G. Cardona, H. Hoenigswald and A. Senn, *Indo-European and Indo-Europeans*, pp. 369–382. Philadelphia: University of Pennsylvania Press.

Rose, H. J. 1959. *A Handbook of Greek Mythology*. New York: E. P. Dutton and Co.

West, M. L. 1997. *The East Face of Helicon: West Asiatic Elements in Greek Poetry and Myth*. Oxford: Oxford University Press.

Woodard, Roger. Forthcoming. *The Cambridge Companion to Greek Myth*. Cambridge: Cambridge University Press.

Yoshida, Atsukiko. 1964. "La structure de l'illustration du bouclier d'Achille." *Revue Belge de Philologie et d'Histoire* 42:5–15.

7 The Gods of Vedic India and Their Indo-European Heritage

Outline of Key Terms and Concepts

1. "Proto-Indo-Iranian" denotes the parent language and culture of the Indo-European Indic and Iranian peoples.
2. Mitanni was a Hurrian kingdom of northern Mesopotamia (Mallory; Dumézil 1986).

    There is evidence for the presence of Indo-Iranian speakers in Mitanni in the fifteenth century BC.

        Some rulers have Indic names: for example, Artatama.

        The name given to an elite group of warriors is the Indic term, *Maryanni*.

            Compare Sanskrit *marya-* 'young warrior'.

        A set of horse-training tablets survives in which Indic numerals and technical vocabulary occur; for example:

            Aika 'one'; *tera* 'three'; *panza* 'five'

            Terms for horse colors: *parita* 'gray'; *babru* 'brown'

        A treaty between Sattiwaza, the king of Mitanni, and Suppiluliuma, a Hittite king, bears the names of Indic gods: Mitra, Uruwana, Indara, Nasattiya.

    Is the Indo-European language attested in Mitanni an early form of Indic or still undifferentiated Indo-Iranian?

3. Indo-Europeans in India

    Indo-Europeans probably had arrived in India by 1500–1200 BC.

    The first written evidence of Indo-European language in India is provided by the *Vedas*.

4. The *Vedas* are collections of hymns preserving the earliest form of Sanskrit.

    Veda is the Sanskrit word for 'knowledge'.

        The Sanskrit tem *veda* is related to Greek *oîda* 'I know'; Latin *video* 'I see'.

    There are four *Vedas*.

        - The *Rig Veda:* from Sanskrit *ṛc-* 'hymn'

            The *Rig Veda* is the earliest of the *Vedas*.

            The *Rig Veda* dates to about 1200 BC.

- The *Sama Veda:* from Sanskrit *sāman-* 'chant'
- The *Atharva Veda:* named after Atharvan, the first fire priest
- The *Yajur Veda:* from Sanskrit *yajus* 'sacrificial text'

The *Vedas* were produced and utilized by the priestly class of Vedic society.

5. The classes of Vedic society

The Sanskrit word for class or caste is *varṇa-* 'color'

The term is used in reference to the color affiliated with each class.

There are three classes in Vedic society: priests, warriors, and goods producers.

Comparable classes occur in the closely related society of the ancient Iranians.

The Avestan term denoting class is *pištra,* literally 'craft' (Benveniste 1969; Dumézil 1992a).

Iranian classes are distinguished by clothing colors of early Indo-European origin.

Priests wear white.

Warriors wear red.

Goods producers wear blue.

The priestly class of India is the Brahmaṇa class (the Brahmins).

The warrior class of India is the Kṣatriya class.

The worker class of India is the Vaiśya class.

Sanskrit *ārya-* is a term that designates collectively the three Indo-European classes of Vedic society.

The Indo-Europeans of India are sometimes termed "Indo-Aryans" by scholars.

Sanskrit *ārya-* is the source of the English word *Aryan.*

A related term in Old Persian, *āriya-*, is the source of the modern name of Persia, *Iran.*

Sanskrit *ārya-* is perhaps in origin an ethnic term of self-designation.

The Śudra class is eventually added as a fourth class.

The Śudra class is not found in the oldest Vedic literature.

The Śudra class is the non-Indo-Aryan element of Vedic society.

6. Divine society in Vedic India also has three divisions (Dumézil 1992b; 1986).

The Adityas are the gods of sovereignty.

The Rudras are the warrior gods.

The Vasus are the gods of goods and wealth.

Sanskrit *vasu-* means 'goods, wealth.'

The chief Vedic deities, spanning the three divisions of divine society, are:

Mitra and Varuṇa (sovereignty)

Indra (war)

The Aśvins or Nasatyas (goods, wealth)

These are the same deities that appear in the Mitanni treaty.

7. The gods of sovereignty (first-function deities; Dumézil 1986)

Mitra

Mitra's name means 'contract'.

Mitra is the god of friendship (see, for example, *Rig Veda* 5.85.7).

Mitra's name becomes a common noun (*mitra-*) meaning 'friend' in later Sanskrit.

Varuṇa

Varuṇa is punisher of sinners.

Varuṇa may inflict sinners with dropsy (see, for example, *Rig Veda* 7.89).

Varuṇa is god of waters (see, for example, *Rig Veda* 7.88).

Varuṇa is possessor of great magic (see, for example, *Rig Veda* 5.85).

Dumézil argues that Mitra and Varuṇa embody the two aspects of the Indo-European first function.

Mitra represents the legal aspect.

Varuṇa represents the magical or magico-religious aspect.

The same two aspects also find expression in the priestly class of human society.

The Brahmins settle legal disputes.

The Brahmins are ascetics with great supernatural power (*tapas-*).

There are also minor first-function deities.

Aryaman

Aryaman is affiliated with Mitra.

Aryaman's name associates him with the society of the Arya.

Aryaman is god of hospitality.

Aryaman is associated with marriage.

Bhaga

Bhaga is also affiliated with Mitra.

Bhaga sees that society's goods are rightly divided among its members.

Bhaga is associated with marriage and with good fortune.

Bhaga's name is cognate with the Old Church Slavic *bogŭ* 'god' and Avestan *baγa-* 'god'.

Dakṣa: a more recent symmetrical counterpart to Aryaman

Dakṣa is affiliated with Varuṇa.

Dakṣa's name means 'skill.'

Dakṣa is concerned with the relationships of divine society.

Dakṣa is associated with creation.

Aṁśa a more recent symmetrical counterpart to Bhaga

Aṁśa is affiliated with Varuṇa.

Aṁśa is a little known figure.

Aṁśa's name means 'portion.'

Aṁśa is distributor of divine benefits and of sacrifices to the gods.

8. Gods of physical power (second-function deities)

Indra

Indra is the warrior god *par excellence.*

Indra's greatest deed is the slaying of the dragon Vṛtra (*Rig Veda* 1.32).

Vṛtra is a dragon that steals cattle and withholds water from the earth.

Indra also kills his father (*Rig Veda* 4.18).

Indra is an Indic reflex of the Indo-European "triple-sinning warrior."

Indra's first-function sin: the murder of Triśiras

Triśiras is a three-headed divine being (the Tricephal).

Triśiras is a Brahmin and chaplain among the gods.

Triśiras is a cousin of the gods.

Indra's second-function sin: the murder of Namuci

The tale is told in the *Mahabharata.*

It is the tale of the murder of an unsuspecting fellow warrior.

Indra's third-function sin: the seduction of the wife of a Brahmin, Gautama

The tale is told in the *Ramayaṇa.*

Gautama castrates Indra with a curse.

Gautama turns his wife to stone.

An Indic-Roman homology: Part 1 (Dumézil 1995:306–307; 1970)

The stories (i) of Indra's murder of the Tricephal and (ii) of Rome's war with Alba Longa under Tullus Hostilius are traditions having a common Indo-European origin.

Indra's murder of Triśiras:

Triśiras is a menace to the well-being of the gods in their rivalry with the demons.

Trita Aptya is the third Aptya brother.

Trita Aptya kills Triśiras (triple enemy and a family member), on behalf of Indra.

- The Aptyas ritually remove the stain of the murder.
- Thereafter, the Aptyas continued to perform such a cleansing function.

Rome's war with Alba Longa during the reign of Tullus Hostilius:

- Alba Longa is Rome's military rival.
- Horatius is the "third brother" of the Horatii.
- Horatius kills the three Curiatii (a triple enemy), on behalf of Tullus Hostilius.
- Horatius kills his sister (a family member).
  - According to some sources, the Curiatii are also family members, being cousins of the Horatii.
- Horatius is cleansed from the stain of her murder by a ritual conducted by his family (the *Tigillum Sororium*).
- The Horatian cleansing ritual continued to be conducted periodically in ancient Rome.

An Indic-Roman homology: Part 2 (Dumézil 1995:307–308; 1970)

The stories (i) of Indra's alliance with Namuci and subsequent execution of him and (ii) of Tullus Hostilius' alliance with Mettius Fuffetius and subsequent execution of him are traditions having a common Indo-European origin.

Indra's alliance with Namuci:

- Former enemies (Indra and Namuci) have agreed to be 'friends' (*sakhāyas*).
- Indra vows not to kill Namuci:
  - By day or by night
  - With anything dry or with anything wet
- Namuci causes Indra to become intoxicated.
- Indra then is robbed of his physical advantages.
- For help, Indra turns to three third-function deities:
- Sarasvati (female) and the twin Aśvins (male)
- By their advice, Indra kills the unsuspecting Namuci at dawn with the foam of a wave.
- Namuci's head is "churned" off with the foam.
  - This is presented as a singularly unusual means of execution in Indic tradition.

Tullus Hostilius' alliance with Mettius Fuffetius:

- Former enemies (Tullus and Mettius) have become allies (*socii*).
- Mettius withdraws his forces from the field during a battle.
- Tullus is robbed of his strength on the right flank.
- For help Tullus calls upon three third-function deities: Ops (female) and Quirinus and Saturnus (both male)

Tullus captures an unsuspecting Mettius and executes him.

Mettius is chained to two teams of horses and his body is split into parts.

This is presented as a singularly unusual means of execution in Roman history (Livy 1.28.11).

A Roman-Indic homology: Part 3 (Puhvel; cf. Dumézil 1994)

Indra and Tullus Hostilius correspond in the two episodes above.

Indra's acts comprise his sins against the first and second functions.

Indra's third-function sin is adultery with the wife of Gautama.

There is no comparable act (third-function sin) associated with Tullus.

In Roman tradition, the third-function sin appears at a later period in the mythic history of Rome, the reign of Tarquinius Superbus, the third of the Tarquin kings.

Sextus is the son of Tarquinius Superbus.

Lucretia is the wife of Tarquinius Collatinus.

Sextus rapes Lucretia.

Lucretia then commits suicide.

Moved by this tragedy, the Roman people revolt and drive the Tarquins out of Rome.

The Roman monarchy comes to an end (about 509 BC).

The Maruts (the gods of physical power continued)

The Maruts are the gods of the storm winds.

The Maruts are Indra's close companions.

The Maruts are known for being self-willed and having an independent spirit.

Sanskrit *svadhā-* means 'independent spirit' (*Rig Veda* 1.165).

Related forms occur in other Indo-European languages.

Early Latin *svodālis* means 'close companion'.

Old Church Slavic *svatŭ* means 'kinsman'.

Viṣṇu

Viṣṇu is a beneficent deity.

Viṣṇu assists Indra in his fight with Vṛtra (*Rig Veda* 4.18).

He is called "three-stepping" Viṣṇu.

In taking his three steps, Viṣṇu creates and supports the spaces of the universe (*Rig Veda* 1.154).

Rudra

Rudra is precursor of the Hindu god Śiva.

Rudra is a god who brings destruction, associated with the untamed wilderness and chaotic forces (*Rig Veda* 1.114).

Rudra is father of the Maruts (*Rig Veda* 2.33).

Viṣṇu and Rudra-Śiva (Dumézil 1983)

In Hinduism, Viṣṇu and Śiva form a contrasting pair.

Viṣṇu is the preserver; chief god of Vaiṣṇavism.

Śiva is the destroyer; chief god of Śaivism.

With Brahma, the creator, they form the Hindu Trimurti.

The contrast of Viṣṇu versus Śiva is already suggested in the *Vedas*.

An hypothesized early Indo-Aryan paradigm is as follows:

Indra is the warrior god who gave victory to the Indo-European invaders of the Indian subcontinent.

Viṣṇu is the god that opened the spaces before them, allowing them to move forward into this new domain.

Rudra is the god inhabiting those wilderness places to be tamed by the newcomers.

Vayu

Vayu is the wind-god.

Vayu's Iranian counterpart is a god of great power.

Parjanya

Parjanya is the rain-god.

Parjanya has important thunder-god counterparts among the Balto-Slavic and Germanic peoples.

Old Russian Perunŭ

Perunŭ is a god of war.

Perunŭ's name is used to translate Latin *Jupiter*, the god whose weapon is the thunderbolt.

In Kiev, Perunŭ's image stood on a hill beneath open sky.

The image is a wooden statue with a head of silver and mustache of gold.

A military leader served as Perunŭ's priest.

Lithuanian Perkunas

Perkunas is a principal deity among the Baltic peoples.

Perkunas is a god of sky and thunder.

Perkunas is a god of war.

Homologous figures occur:

- Latvian Perkuns
- Old Norse Fjörgyn(n)

Fjörgyn is an androgynous deity.

Fjörgyn is the mother of Thor (the god of thunder, whose weapon is the thunderbolt).

9. Gods of fertility and wealth (third-function deities)

The Aśvins or Nasatyas, the divine twins, are the chief representatives of this group.

In the treaty from Mitanni, they are called the *Nasattiya.*

The meaning of the Sanskrit name *Nāsatyās* is uncertain.

A possible meaning is "rescuers," an activity for which the Aśvins are praised in the *Rig Veda.*

Another possible meaning is "ones who recover"; the Aśvins recover the light each morning.

The Aśvins drive a three-wheeled chariot, leading the Dawn (Uṣas) across the sky each morning.

The name *Aśvins* is derived from the Sanskrit word *aśva-* 'horse'.

Numerous cognates exist, such as Latin *equus;* Greek *híppos;* Old Irish *ech;* Avestan *aspa-;* Tocharian A *yuk;* among others.

These Indic gods are in Sanskrit the *Aśvināu,* 'the two horsemen'.

The Aśvins are associated with the ocean.

The Aśvins rescue the drowning man Bhujyu, with their flying boat having one hundred oars (*Rig Veda* 1.116).

The Aśvins and the Dioscuri (Nagy 1990)

The Aśvins are collectively called "the Sons of Dyaus."

Dyaus is descended from the Proto-Indo-European sky-god **Dyeus* (see Figure 3.1).

His name, Dyaus Pitar, is cognate to that of Zeus Pater and Jupiter.

Vedic Dyaus has become a minor figure, with many of his sky-god features being assigned to Indra.

Dyaus is closely affiliated with Pṛthivi, 'Earth', who is presented as his wife (*Rig Veda* 1.160).

The Aśvins are also said to have been "born differently" (*Rig Veda* 5.73.4).

One of the Aśvins is the son of Dyaus.

The other is the son of Sumakhas, 'Good Warrior', apparently a mortal.

The Aśvins form a contrasting pair.

The Aśvins contrast as immortal vs. mortal.

One of the Aśvins is fathered by Dyaus.

The other is fathered by Sumakhas.

The Aśvins contrast as light vs. dark.

One of the Aśvins is called "the son of day."

The other is called "the son of night."

One of the Aśvins is said to be the Morning Star.

    - The other is said to be the Evening Star.
- The Dioscuri are the "Boys/Sons of Zeus."
  - The Dioscuri are Castor and Polydeuces (or Pollux).
  - The mother of the Dioscuri is Leda, wife of the Spartan king Tyndareus.
  - The Dioscuri have two sisters, Helen and Clytemnestra.
- There is a distinction between the two Dioscuri.
  - Polydeuces is the son of Zeus (and Helen the daughter of Zeus).
  - Castor is the son of Tyndareus (and Clytemnestra the daughter of Tyndareus).
- The Dioscuri are associated with horses.
  - The Dioscuri are called the *leukópoloi* 'bright horses'.
  - When the Dioscuri are borrowed into Roman tradition, they are presented as fighting on the side of the Roman cavalry.
- The Dioscuri are associated with boats and mariners.
  - The Dioscuri are said to be present in St. Elmo's Fire: electrical discharges that occur at the higher portions of sailing vessels during storms.
- The Dioscuri are involved in conflict with the brothers Idas and Lynceus.
  - Idas and Lynceus are the sons of Aphareus, brother of the Spartan king Tyndareus.
  - There are at least two causes for conflict (Apollodorus 3.11.2).
    - One concerns the daughters of Leucippus.
      - Leucippus, also brother of Tyndareus, has two daughters, Phoebe and Hilaera.
      - Castor and Polydeuces abduct the sisters and take them as their wives.
      - Idas and Lynceus insult Castor and Polydeuces for their abduction of the women.
      - According to some sources, Idas and Lynceus were to be married to the abducted Phoebe and Hilaera.
    - Another concerns the theft of cattle.
      - The two sets of brothers steal cattle together.
      - Idas and Lynceus cheat Castor and Polydeuces out of their share.
  - Castor and Polydeuces fight with Idas and Lynceus (Pindar *Nemean Ode* 10.49–91).
    - Idas and Lynceus attack Castor.
    - Polydeuces stabs Lynceus.
    - Zeus strikes Idas with a thunderbolt.

Polydeuces finds the dying Castor and grieves.

Zeus allows his son Polydeuces to share his immortal life with Tyndareus's son Castor.

The Dioscuri form a contrasting pair.

The Dioscuri contrast as immortal vs. mortal.

One of the Dioscuri is fathered by Zeus.

The other is fathered by Tyndareus.

In sharing a single immortal existence, the Dioscuri contrast as life vs. death.

The contrast is described in two ways:

- Both of the Dioscuri spend one day among the dead, the next day with the gods of Olympus, and so on.
- One of the Dioscuri spends one day among the dead while the other is among the gods; the next day they exchange positions, and so on.

The Aśvins and the Dioscuri are cognate figures; they are divine twins having a common Indo-European origin.

Each set of twins is collectively referred to as the "sons of the sky god" (Dyaus or Zeus).

Only one member of each set is actually the son of the sky god; the other was fathered by a mortal warrior.

The two sets of twins constitute similarly contrasting pairs:

- The Aśvins: immortal vs. mortal; light vs. dark
- The Dioscuri: immortal vs. mortal; life vs. death

Each set of twins is associated with mariners and boats.

Each set of twins is associated with horses.

The adopted son of the Aśvins is Puṣan (*Rig Veda* 10.85).

Puṣan is a deity with several functions (Puhvel; Keith pp. 106–108).

Puṣan is god of roads and journeys (*Rig Veda* 1.42).

Puṣan is charioteer of the sun; i.e. Puṣan conveys a divine being, the sun, from one horizon to the other.

Puṣan protects animals and is closely associated with cattle (*Rig Veda* 6.54; 10.17).

Puṣan is associated with goats: his chariot is drawn by goats; his goat leads the Vedic sacrificial horse.

Puṣan is presented as a messenger (*Rig Veda* 6.58).

Puṣan serves as a psychopomp (*Rig Veda* 10.17).

Greek Hermes shares these functions.

Consider also the Greek god Pan (earlier Paon).

Pan is a son of Hermes (*Homeric Hymn to Pan*).

Pan is god of flocks and shepherds.

Pan's lower body is that of a goat.

**Pauson* can be reconstructed as a still earlier form of Pan's name.

Greek *Pan* and Sanskrit *Puṣan* would then be linguistic cognates.

By this analysis, the two gods, Indic Puṣan and Greek Pan/Hermes, have a single origin in a common ancestral god.

Another tradition identifies the Aśvins as sons of the solar god Vivasva(n)t (Puhvel; Dumézil 1929).

Vivasvat is married to Saraṇyu (daughter of Tvaṣṭṛ, the smith god).

Vivasvat and Saraṇyu produce the twins Yama (male) and Yami (female).

Yami attempts to seduce Yama (*Rig Veda* 10.10).

Yama, the first mortal, becomes king of the dead (*Rig Veda* 10.14).

Saraṇyu then produces a clone of herself, Savarṇa ('having the same appearance'; *Rig Veda* 10.17).

Saraṇyu changes herself into a horse and runs away, leaving the clone in her place.

Vivasvat and Savarṇa produce a son, Manu (the father of humankind).

Vivasvat then changes himself into a horse and finds Saraṇyu.

In horse form, they produce offspring: the Aśvins.

Compare the Arcadian tradition of Poseidon and Demeter mating in horse form, producing twin offspring.

Vivasvat and Ixion

Ixion is king of Thessaly in Greece and, according to some, the brother of Coronis.

Ixion attempts to seduce Hera.

Zeus creates a clone of Hera from a cloud.

Ixion has intercourse with the cloud and is caught by Zeus.

Zeus straps Ixion to a revolving wheel of fire that passes continually through the heavens.

Zeus causes Ixion to drink a potion giving him immortality; his punishment is thus eternal.

This image of Ixion suggests an association of the tradition with a solar deity.

The cloud gives birth to Centaurus.

Centaurus has intercourse with mares of Mt. Pelion.

From their union, the race of the Centaurs is born.

Centaurs are male creatures having the upper body of a man and the lower body of a horse.

There are several similarities between these Vedic and Greek traditions:

- A solar deity has intercourse with the clone of a goddess.
- The resulting offspring is the progenitor of a new race of beings:

  Manu: Humankind

  Centaurus: Centaurs
- The same solar deity is progenitor of beings with horse affinities: the Aśvins and Centaurs.

Centaurs

Centaurs live in remote regions, on the fringe of human settlement.

Centaurs are savage beings that are at the same time educators and healers.

Centaurs are lecherous creatures.

Centaurs are affiliated with nymphs, especially those of Mt. Pelion.

Compare the Gandharvas of Indic tradition:

- Gandharvas are spirits of nature.
- Gandharvas have the head of a horse and body of a man.
- Gandharvas are lecherous creatures.
- Gandharvas are affiliated with the Apsaras, nymph-like beings inhabiting the waters and forests.

Greek *kéntauros* ('Centaur') and Sanskrit *gandharvas* bear a close semantic and phonetic similarity.

Compare also:

Avestan *gandərəva-*, the name of a monster

Shughni (an Iranian language) *žindūrv* 'werewolf'

Latin *Februus*, a Roman god of the dead

Greek *kéntauros* ('Centaur') and Sanskrit *gandharvas* do not form a strict cognate set.

Their similarity may be the result of borrowing rather than of common inheritance.

10. Among the Indo-Aryan deities are trifunctional gods, deities associated with all three functions (Dumézil 1995:118–120).

Agni: the fire god

Sanskrit *agni-* means 'fire'; Indo-European cognates include Latin *ignis;* Old Church Slavic *ognĭ;* Old Lithuanian *ungnis.*

Agni is invoked on behalf of priests, warriors, and agriculturalists (*Rig Veda* 8.71).

Agni is invoked together with each of the three elements of divine society—Adityas, Indra, Aśvins—for protection of the worshipper (*Atharva Veda* 19.16).

Apaṁ Napat ('Child of the Waters') is the fire within the waters (*Rig Veda* 2.35).

At times, Apaṁ Napat is identified with Agni.

Apaṁ Napat is at least of Proto-Indo-Iranian origin.

Avestan Apam Napat is an obscure but important deity.

Śri: goddess of prosperity

At the Aśvamedha (the horse sacrifice for a king), three of the king's wives anoint the body of the sacrificial horse to give the sacrificer prosperity (*śri-*).

The first wife anoints the front of the horse to bring spiritual force (first-function element).

The second wife anoints the middle portion to bring physical force (second-function element).

The third wife anoints the hind portion to bring livestock (third-function element).

11. The Roman Equus October and the Vedic Aśvamedha: Cognate rituals (Dumézil 1996:215–227).

The Roman horse sacrifice: the Equus October

The Equus October is a sacrifice offered to Mars on the Ides of October.

The sacrifice takes place on the Campus Martius.

The officiating priest is probably the Flamen Martialis.

The selection and immolation of the sacrificial victim entails the following:

- A chariot race is held.
- The right-hand member of the winning team of horses is chosen to be sacrificed.
- The horse is killed with a javelin.

A division of the victim then occurs:

- The horse's tail is cut off.

The tail is carried to the Regia (the king's residence) before the blood can drain out.

Blood from the tail is sprinkled on the king's hearth.

- The horse's head is cut off.

A fight for possession of the head is waged by people from two areas of Rome:

People from the area of the Sacra Via

The Sacra Via is the oldest street in Rome, running through the Forum to and beyond the Regia.

If these people gain the head, it is mounted on the Regia.

People from the Subura

The Subura is a district known for its grittiness and brothels.

If these people gain the head, it is mounted on a tower, the Turris Mamilia.

The tower stood in the Subura.

The tower was named for the Mamilii, an important family from Tusculum.

- The horse's head is decorated with small loaves of bread.

This is said to be a ritual conducted for the sake of a good grain harvest, or in thanksgiving for such a harvest.

The Vedic horse sacrifice: the Aśvamedha

The Aśvamedha is the subject of Rig Vedic hymns; for example *Rig Veda* 1.162; 1.163; 10.56.

Detailed information about the Aśvamedha, however, is provided by the *Yajur Veda*.

The Aśvamedha is a sacrifice of the warrior (Kṣatriya) class.

At an early period the sacrifice was offered to Indra.

The sacrifice is offered on behalf of a warrior-king who wishes to gain preeminence among kings.

The selection of the sacrificial victim entails the following:

- A chariot race is held.
- The right-hand member of the winning team of horses is chosen to be sacrificed.

The chosen horse is allowed to roam freely for a period of one year.

A member of the king's household follows the horse to protect it from foreign rulers whose lands the horse traverses.

If the horse is captured, the king's sacrificial effort has been foiled.

If the horse survives the year, the sacrificial ritual proceeds.

The ritual division and immolation of the victim occur as follows:

- The horse's body is marked into three sections (front, middle and hind).

- Each section is anointed by one of the king's wives to provide the king with advantages that span the three functions.

  Anointing the front of the horse brings the king *tejas-* (spiritual force).

  Anointing the middle of the horse brings the king *indriya-* (physical force).

  Anointing the hind portion of the horse brings the king *paśu-* (livestock).

- The king's wives attach golden beads to the hair of the horses head and tail.
- Smaller sacrificial victims are attached to the horse's body, with prominence given to bindings on the head and tail.

  Each smaller victim is dedicated to a god.

  Indra receives a victim attached at the head or tail.

- The horse is immolated by suffocation.

Homologous elements characterize the Roman and Vedic horse sacrifices.

The Aśvamedha and the Equus October are both sacrifices to the war god, made for the benefit of the king.

The victim of the Aśvamedha and that of the Equus October are similarly selected, and in both rituals the victim's body is apportioned into three parts.

The Aśvamedha and the Equus October both entail risks that may jeopardize the efficacy of the sacrifice.

The risks involve movement of the victim through time and space.

The designated victim of the Vedic sacrifice travels through the wilderness for one year.

The severed tail, and, if all goes well, head of the Roman horse travel to the king's residence.

The king depends upon others to ensure the success of the sacrifice.

The Vedic king depends upon a member of his household to protect the sacrificial horse from foreign elements and deliver it to him.

The Roman king depends on representatives of the Sacra Via to defend the horse's severed head from a foreign force, represented by the Subura and its Turris Mamilia, and to deliver it to him.

The Roman king also depends upon one to bring the tail of the horse to the hearth of the Regia sufficiently quickly so that the blood will not have drained from it.

Bibliography and Further Reading

Alexinsky, G. 1989. "Slavonic Mythology." In *The New Larousse Encyclopedia of Mythology*, pp. 281–298. New York: Crescent Books.

Benveniste, Émile. 1969. *Le vocabulaire des institutions indo-européennes*. Paris: Les Éditions de Minuit.

Bonnefoy, Yves. 1991. *Mythologies*. Chicago: University of Chicago Press.

Bowker, John. 1997. *The Oxford Dictionary of World Religions*. Oxford: Oxford University Press.

Boyer, Régis. 1991a. "Slavic Myths, Rites, and Gods." In Bonnefoy 1991, pp. 295–302.

_____. 1991b. "Baltic Myths and Religious Categories." In Bonnefoy 1991, pp. 305–306.

_____. 1991c. "The Kinship of Slavic and Norse Mythologies." In Bonnefoy 1991, pp. 302–305.

Doniger O'Flaherty, Wendy. 1981. *The Rig Veda*. London: Penguin Books.

Dumézil, Georges. 1996. *Archaic Roman Religion*. Reprint edition. Baltimore: Johns Hopkins University Press.

_____. 1995. *Mythe et épopée I. II. III.* Paris: Gallimard.

_____. 1994. "Les trois péchés des Tarquins, père et fils." In *Le Roman des jumeaux*, pp. 271–277. Paris: Gallimard.

_____. 1992a. "Les trois fonctions sociales et cosmiques." In *Mythes et dieux des Indo-Européens*, pp. 81–116 [originally published in 1958]. Paris: Flammarion.

_____. 1992b. "Les théologies triparties." In *Mythes et dieux des Indo-Européens*, pp. 117–154 [originally published in 1958]. Paris: Flammarion.

_____. 1988. *Mitra-Varuna*. New York: Zone Books.

_____. 1986. *Les dieux souverains des Indo-Européens*. Paris: Gallimard.

_____. 1983. *The Stakes of the Warrior*. Berkeley and Los Angeles: The University of California Press.

_____. 1970. *The Destiny of the Warrior*. Translated by A. Hiltebeitel. Chicago: University of Chicago Press.

_____. 1929. *Le problème des centaures*. Paris: Annales du Musée Guimet.

Keith, Arthur. 1998. *The Religion and Philosophy of the Vedas and the Upanishads*. Reprint edition. Delhi: Motilal Banarsidass Publishers.

Mallory, J. P. 1989. *In Search of the Indo-Europeans*. London: Thames and Hudson.

Mallory, J. P. and D. Q. Adams. 1997. *Encyclopedia of Indo-European Culture*. London and Chicago: Fitzroy Dearborn Publishers.

Nagy, Gregory. 1990. *Greek Mythology and Poetics*. Ithaca: Cornell University Press.

Polomé, Edgar. 1997. "Centaur." In Mallory and Adams 1997, p. 103.

Puhvel, Jaan. 1987. "The Concepts 'Indo-European' and 'Indo-Iranian' "; "Vedic India." In *Comparative Mythology*, pp. 33–67. Baltimore: Johns Hopkins University Press.

Schnapp, Alain. 1991. "Centaurs." In Bonnefoy 1991, pp. 451–452.

8 The Mahabharata and Its Indo-European Heritage

Outline of Key Terms and Concepts

1. There are two epics of ancient India.

    The Mahabharata

    The *Mahabharata* is approximately eight times longer than Homer's *Iliad* and *Odyssey* combined.

    The Mahabharata consists of eighteen books, centered on the eighteen-day battle of Kurukṣetra.

    The Ramayaṇa

    The term "Sanskrit" first appears in *The Ramayaṇa: saṁskṛta-* 'purified'.

    The historical setting of the epics is probably the early to mid-first millennium BC.

    The epics acquired their approximate present form in the first centuries AD.

2. *The Mahabharata:* A closer look

    Book One: *The Book of Beginning*

    The initial one-third of Book One consists of miscellaneous stories, loosely connected.

    Then follows a genealogy of the principal characters:

    Manu: the son of Vivasvat and Savarṇa

    Iḷa

    Pururavas

    Pururavas marries the Apsara Urvaśi.

    Urvaśi marries Pururavas on the condition that she will never see him unclothed.

    The Gandharvas cause a disturbance in the house of Pururavas and Urvaśi one night.

    When Pururavas gets up to investigate, the Gandharvas cause lightning to flash.

    Urvaśi sees Pururavas unclothed and she disappears.

    This story is preserved in one of the *Brahmaṇas*, commentaries on the *Vedas*.

    One encounters the couple in the *Rig Veda* only after Urvaśi has left Pururavas (*Rig Veda* 10.95).

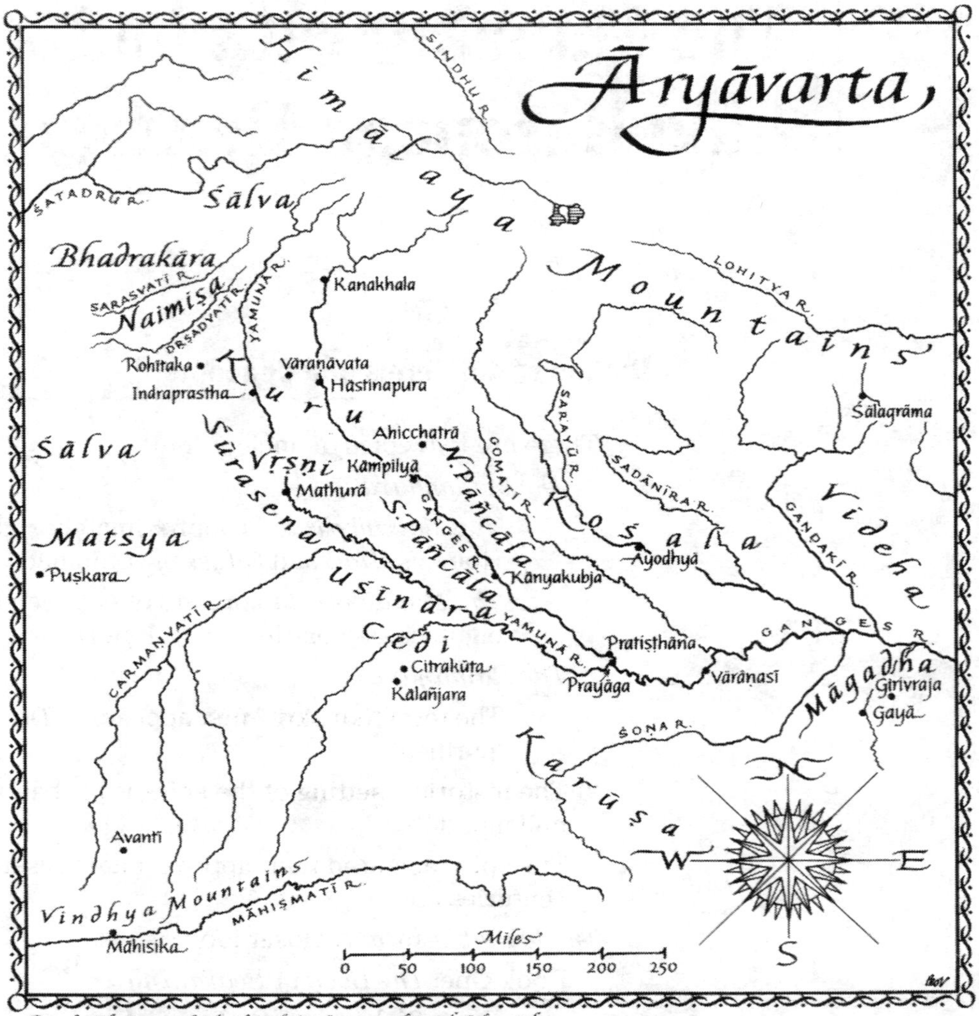

Based on The Historical Atlas of South Asia, courtesy of Joseph Schwartzberg, Department of Geography, The University of Minnesota.

Map 8–1 The India of the Mahabharata

Yayati: a descendant of Pururavas

- Yayati is a king and famed ascetic.
- Indra throws Yayati out of heaven because of the conceit that he shows concerning his practice of austerities.
- Yayati is a trifunctional figure (Dumézil 1973; 1995:911–1045).
  - Yayati experiences conflict with his sons.
  - Yayati has four grandsons: sons of his daughter Madhavi, whose name is derived from Sanskrit *madhu-* (from Proto-Indo-European **med^hu-*), a word denoting an intoxicating beverage.
  - Each of Yayati's grandsons is affiliated with one of the Indo-European functions.

One is called "the lord of gifts," named Vasumanas (third function).

The next is a hero (second function).

The next is a friend of truth and justice (first function; legal aspect).

The next is a devoted sacrificer (first function; magico-religious aspect).

When Yayati falls from heaven, he encounters his four grandsons, kings, engaged in sacrifice.

The four kings transfer their own (trifunctional) merits to Yayati, who is thus restored to heaven.

Dumézil compares Yayati to the homologous Celtic figure Eochaid Feidlech, an Irish king.

Eochaid Feidlech fights against his sons.

Eochaid Feidlech has a daughter Medb, whose name means 'drunk' or 'intoxicating' (from Proto-Indo-European *med^hu-*).

Medb has multiple husbands linked to the three functions by the requirements she places upon marriage. Her husbands must be:

- "Without jealousy" (as a judge must be; first function)
- "Without fear" (as a warrior must be; second function)
- "Without greed" (as a goods producer must be; third function)

Duḥṣanta: a descendant of Yayati

While hunting in the forest, Duḥṣanta visits the home of the ascetic Kaṇva.

Kaṇva is away gathering fruit.

Duḥṣanta finds there instead a young woman, Śakuntala.

Śakuntala identifies herself as the daughter of Kaṇva.

Duḥṣanta is not convinced, saying that he knows Kaṇva has taken a vow of celibacy (and that Kaṇva would be more faithful to such a vow than even the god Dharma).

Śakuntala explains:

There was once a powerful Brahmin named Viśvamitra.

Viśvamitra had grown enormously powerful through the practice of his austere lifestyle.

Indra fears Viśvamitra's power.

Indra sends the Apsara Menaka to seduce Viśvamitra and rob him of the power (*tapas-*) generated by his ascetic practices.

Menaka does so; she conceives and gives birth to a baby girl, Śakuntala.

- Menaka abandons the baby, who is cared for by birds until found and taken in by Kaṇva.
- Śakuntala's father (Viśvamitra) had been born a member of the Kṣatriya class, to which Duḥṣanta also belongs.
- Duḥṣanta and Śakuntala can thus marry; he proposes, explaining the eight forms of marriage, six of which are lawful for the Kṣatriya class.
- They choose the *gandharva* style of marriage: immediate marriage simply by mutual consent of the man and woman.
- The Indo-Aryan *gandharva* form of marriage finds a functional counterpart in the Roman marital practice called *usus*.
- Both are likely descended from a Proto-Indo-European marriage form (Dumézil 1979).
- Duḥṣanta and Śakuntala have a son, Bharata.

Śaṁtanu: a descendant of Bharata

- Śaṁtanu marries Ganga, goddess of the river Ganges.
- Ganga had taken on human form in order to birth eight (or nine) cursed gods.
  - Dyaus and seven (or eight) other Vasus stole the cow of the Brahmin Vasiṣṭha, which was desired by the wife of Dyaus.
  - Vasiṣṭha discovered the thieves and cursed them with a mortal existence.
  - Ganga agreed to bear the gods and to destroy the first seven (or eight) following birth (and so shorten their misery in a human life form).
  - The last-born, Dyaus, must not be destroyed; he was cursed to live a long life without producing children of his own.
- After the birth of the last child (Dyaus in human form), Ganga explains to Śaṁtanu who she is and why she has taken human form; she then disappears along with the boy, who is called Devavrata and Gangeya.
- The son grows up and is reunited with his father Śaṁtanu; the son will be called Bhiṣma.
- Śaṁtanu desires to marry Satyavati, the adopted daughter of the king of a tribe of fisher folk.
- Her father will permit Satyavati to marry Śaṁtanu only upon the condition that the son she will bear will become king after Śaṁtanu and that he will be Śaṁtanu's heir.
- Śaṁtanu is heartbroken; he cannot agree to the condition because Bhiṣma, his son by Ganga, would then be cut off from the throne.

- For the sake of his father's happiness, Bhiṣma voluntarily renounces the throne and takes a vow of celibacy.
- For this unselfish act of love, Śaṁtanu gives Bhiṣma a special blessing—the gift of a long life that no one can take from him against his will.
- Śaṁtanu marries Satyavati and they have two sons.

Citrangada: older son of Śaṁtanu and Satyavati

- Śaṁtanu dies.
- Citrangada ascends to the throne.
- Citrangada then fights many battles and defeats all who oppose him.
- Citrangada fights against the king of the Gandharvas, also named Citrangada.
  - Their duel, a magical fight, lasts for three years.
  - Citrangada, son of Śaṁtanu, is killed.

Vicitravirya: younger son of Śaṁtanu and Satyavati

- When Citrangada dies, Vicitravirya is too young to take the throne.
- Bhiṣma governs until Vicitravirya comes of age.
- Bhiṣma takes by force three wives for Vicitravirya: Amba, Ambika, and Ambalika, daughters of the king of the Kaśis.
  - Amba had already chosen a husband, King Śalva.
  - Bhiṣma allows Amba to return to Śalva.
  - Ambika and Ambalika marry Vicitravirya.
- Vicitravirya dies, childless, seven years later.
- Satyavati begs Bhiṣma to forsake his vow and to father children by Vicitravirya's widows, providing an heir to the throne.
- Bhiṣma refuses.
- Bhiṣma directs Satyavati to find a virtuous Brahmin to engender children by Vicitravirya's widows.

Vyasa: son of Satyavati

- By an unusual sequence of events, Satyavati had been conceived within a fish.
- When the fish was caught and cleaned, the infant Satyavati was found within it and adopted by the fisher king.
- Because of her development within a fish, she was plagued with a fishy odor.
- When Satyavati was a young girl, she allowed a powerful Brahmin, Paraśara, to make love to her, and in exchange he took away her fishy odor and replaced it with a fragrance.

The child born from their union became a great seer, the hermit Vyasa, the compiler of *The Mahabharata.*

Satyavati now recruits her son Vyasa to provide her with grandchildren by the widows of Vicitravirya.

Vyasa first visits Ambika.

Ambika finds his unkempt appearance repugnant.

Ambika closes her eyes.

Because Ambika would not look on him, Vyasa announces that her child, Dhṛtaraṣṭra, will be born blind.

Vyasa next visits Ambalika.

Ambalika turns pale when she sees Vyasa.

Vyasa announces that her child, Paṇḍu, will thus have a sickly pallor all of his life.

Vyasa then visits Ambika again.

Ambika substitutes in her place a Śudra slave.

The slave is not repelled by Vyasa.

Vyasa announces that her child, Vidura, will become a man of great wisdom.

Bhiṣma raises the three sons of the widows.

The Paṇḍavas and the Kauravas

Paṇḍu grows up to be king.

Dhṛtaraṣṭra, , the oldest of the sons fathered by Vyasa, is denied the throne because of his blindness.

Vidura, the youngest, is denied the throne because of his mixed ethnicity.

Paṇḍu marries two princesses:

- Kunti: his first wife
- Madri: his second wife

Dhṛtaraṣṭra, marries the princess Gandhari, and she conceives.

While hunting one day, Paṇḍu shoots a buck and a doe having intercourse.

The buck is a Brahmin who had taken on the form of a deer.

The Brahmin curses Paṇḍu: he will die if he ever makes love to a woman.

Dejected, Paṇḍu withdraws to live in the forest with his wives, facing a life without children; the throne passes to Dhṛtaraṣṭra.

Kunti reveals to Paṇḍu that she is able to summon a god to father a child with her.

As a girl, she had served a Brahmin, Durvasas.

- The Brahmin had taught her a mantra that would bring the gods to her.
- Paṇḍu tells Kunti to call Dharma (the god whose name means 'law').
    - By Dharma, Kunti conceives Paṇḍu's first son, Yudhiṣṭhira.
- Paṇḍu tells Kunti to call Vayu (the wind-god).
    - By Vayu, Kunti conceives Paṇḍu's second son, Bhima.
- Paṇḍu tells Kunti to call Indra.
    - By Indra, Kunti conceives Paṇḍu's third son, Arjuna.
- Paṇḍu asks Kunti to assist Madri in summoning a god.
    - Madri calls the Aśvins.
    - By the Aśvins, Madri conceives twin sons for Paṇḍu: Nakula and Sahadeva.

After a pregnancy of two years, Gandhari, wife of Dhṛtaraṣṭra, has still not given birth.

When Gandhari hears of the birth of Paṇḍu's first son, she aborts the fetus she has carried.

- The fetus has the appearance of a ball of clotted blood.
- Gandhari intends to throw it out, but Vyasa prevents her.
- Vyasa instructs her to sprinkle it with cold water, whereupon the ball segments into one hundred embryos, and to place each embryo into a pot.
- From these pots, one hundred sons are born over a period of a month.
    - Duryodhana: the first-born (born the same day as Bhima)
    - Duḥśasana: the second-born

One spring day, Paṇḍu is overcome by desire for Madri.

- Making love to her, he dies.
- Madri throws herself upon Paṇḍu's funeral pyre, having left her twin sons in the care of Kunti.

The five sons of Paṇḍu (the Paṇḍavas) and the one hundred sons of Dhṛtaraṣṭra (the Kauravas) are raised together by Bhiṣma in Hastinapura, the city of the king.

- The two sets of cousins never get along.
    - Bhima is a constant source of irritation to the Kauravas.
    - Duryodhana tries to kill the sons of Paṇḍu on several occasions.
- The Brahmin Droṇa arrives and becomes the teacher of the cousins.

- Karṇa, a stranger, arrives and is befriended by the Kauravas.
  - Karṇa was raised by a chariot-driver, Adhiratha.
  - In truth, Karṇa is the son of Kunti.
    - Upon learning the Brahmin's mantra as a girl, Kunti had summoned Surya (the sun-god) to come to her.
    - Surya fathered a child, Karṇa, by her.
    - Kunti abandoned the child.
    - Adhiratha found Karṇa and cared for him as his foster son.

When the cousins are grown, Duryodhana persuades Dhṛtaraṣṭra to send the sons of Paṇḍu and Kunti away from the royal city of Hastinapura to live in Varaṇavata.

- There, Duryodhana has built a house for them.
- The house is constructed with lacquer and other highly combustible materials.
- Duryodhana sends his evil minister Purocana to live with the Paṇḍavas, and instructs him to set the house on fire one night as they sleep.
- The Paṇḍavas realize that the house is a trap and build a secret cellar in which they sleep at night.
- After a year, the Paṇḍavas decide the time is right for them to set the house preemptively ablaze with Purocana in it.
- Kunti and the sons of Paṇḍu substitute a woman and her five sons for themselves, set the fire, and secretly escape.
- The bodies of seven people are found in the ashes of the house; Duryodhana believes he has rid himself of the problem of the Paṇḍavas.

Following the fire, the Paṇḍavas wander in the forest, disguised as student Brahmins, having many adventures.

The wandering Paṇḍavas come one day to the land of the Pañcalas, ruled by king Drupada.

- Drupada's daughter, Draupadi, is having her *svayaṁvara* (bridegroom-selection ceremony).
- Arjuna enters the archery competition that will determine whom Draupadi will marry.
- Arjuna wins and announces to Kunti, his mother, that he has won a prize.
- Not realizing the prize is a bride, Kunti tells Arjuna that he must share the prize with his brothers.
- Draupadi becomes the common wife of all five of the sons of Paṇḍu.

- When the Kauravas discover that the Paṇḍavas are still alive and now allied with the Pañcalas, they are despondent and terror-stricken.
    - Duryodhana proposes numerous seditious schemes to best the Paṇḍavas.
    - Karṇa presses for open war with the Paṇḍavas.
- Bhiṣma persuasively opposes war.
    - Dhṛtaraṣṭra divides his kingdom with the Paṇḍavas, giving them the Khandava Tract for their own kingdom.
    - The Paṇḍavas found their capital city of Indraprastha.
    - Yudhiṣṭhira rules as king of the Paṇḍavas.
- Arjuna takes another wife, his cousin Subhadra, by bride-abduction.
    - Subhadra is the sister of Kṛṣṇa, close companion of the Paṇḍavas.
    - Subhadra and Kṛṣṇa are children of Vasudeva, the brother of Kunti.
    - Kṛṣṇa is said to be Viṣṇu in human form.

Book Two: *The Book of the Assembly Hall*

- Yudhiṣṭhira and the kingdom of the Paṇḍavas raid the kingdom of Magadha.
    - Magadha is ruled by King Jarasaṁdha; his general is Śiśupala of Cedi.
    - Jarasaṁdha and Śiśupala have made war on and captured various rajanyas (warrior kings).
    - Jarasaṁdha and Śiśupala plan to offer the rajanyas as victims to their god Śiva.
    - Kṛṣna advises Yudhiṣṭhira to destroy Jarasaṁdha.
        - Kṛṣna is said to be Viṣṇu in human form and the rulers of Magadha are devoted to Śiva.
            - Note that Viṣṇu and Śiva are opposing figures.
    - Kṛṣna, Bhima and Arjuna travel to Magadha; and Bhima kills Jarasaṁdha.
        - Śiśupala survives.
    - A great ceremony is held in honor of Yudhiṣṭhira, at which he will be recognized as preeminent among kings.
        - Kṛṣṇa is chosen to be the guest of honor at the festival.
        - Śiśupala objects loudly to the choice and issues a challenge.
        - Before Kṛṣṇa and Śiśupala fight, Kṛṣṇa enumerates five sins perpetrated by Śiśupala (Dumézil 1983).

1. Śiśupala burned down the city of the Yadavas (the tribe of Kṛṣṇa) while the king and others were away from the city.
2. Śiśupala killed and captured unsuspecting rajanyas while they were at leisure on Mt. Raivataka.
3. Śiśupala stole the sacrificial horse after it had been set free in the Aśvamedha for Vasudeva (Kṛṣṇa's father).
4. Śiśupala abducted the woman who was to become the wife of Babhru.
5. Śiśupala abducted the bride Bhadra, disguising himself as her husband.

Śiśupala responds by insulting Rukmini, the wife of Kṛṣṇa.

Kṛṣṇa decapitates Śiśupala with his discus.

A radiant essence escapes from the decapitated body of Śiśupala and is absorbed by Kṛṣṇa.

Though a great and good king, Yudhiṣṭhira has a weakness: he has a passion for gambling and gambles badly (compare *Rig Veda* 10.34).

The Kauravas invite Yudhiṣṭhira to a dicing match at the court of Dhṛtaraṣṭra .

Yudhiṣṭhira accepts; upon arrival he discovers he will play against Duryodhana's uncle, Śakuni.

Śakuni, the brother of Gandhari, is a professional gambler.

Throw after throw, Yudhiṣṭhira losses to Śakuni; his losses include:

- 100,000 pieces of gold
- His royal chariot
- 1,000 elephants
- 100,000 female slaves
- 100,000 male slaves
- 400 coffers of gold
- His great wealth
- His livestock
- His city, country, and subjects

One-by-one, Yudhiṣṭhira stakes and loses his brothers: Nakula, Sahadeva, Arjuna, and Bhima.

Yudhiṣṭhira stakes and loses himself.

Yudhiṣṭhira stakes and loses Draupadi, the wife of the Paṇḍavas.

Bedlam breaks out in the gaming hall after the loss of Draupadi.

Bhima swears he will drink the blood of Duḥśasana and break the thigh of Duryodhana.

A portent of ominous animal sounds is heard in the hall.

Dhṛtaraṣṭra frees the Paṇḍavas at the request of Draupadi.

With Dhṛtaraṣṭra's blessing, the Paṇḍavas will return home to their kingdom and their wealth.

After the Paṇḍavas leave Hastinapura, Duryodhana persuades Dhṛtaraṣṭra to let him continue the dicing match.

A messenger overtakes Yudhiṣṭhira with Dhṛtaraṣṭra's command to return to the gaming hall.

The Paṇḍavas return for a final throw; Śakuni explains the stake:

The losers will go into exile in the forest for twelve years, dressed in deerskin.

In the thirteenth year of exile, the losers will disguise themselves and live in society.

If they are recognized, the losers must then return to the forest for another twelve years of exile.

If they are not recognized, they will regain their kingdom.

Yudhiṣṭhira loses and the Paṇḍavas with Draupadi go into exile.

Book Three: *The Book of the Forest*

Book Three recounts the experiences and adventures of the Paṇḍavas during the first twelve years of exile, which include the following:

- Arjuna struggles with Śiva, disguised as a mountain man, and wins the Paśupati missile.
- Arjuna ascends to heaven.
- Bhima does battle with the Rakṣasas.

  The Rakṣasas constitute a class of demons.

  The Rakṣasas are shape-shifters who can take on human and animal forms.
- Arjuna rejoins his brothers and they battle the Gandharvas, who have captured Duryodhana.
- Yudhiṣṭhira frees Duryodhana, who is thereby greatly shamed.
- Draupadi is abducted and rescued by Bhima and Arjuna.

Book Four: *The Book of Viraṭa*

Book Four recounts the events of the thirteenth year of exile.

In disguise, the sons of Paṇḍu and their wife Draupadi serve Virāṭa, the king of Matsya.

Yudhiṣṭhira disguises himself as a Brahmin who serves as Virāṭa's games master.

Bhima disguises himself as a butcher/cook who performs as a gladiator-wrestler.

Draupadi disguises herself as a chambermaid.

Sahadeva disguises himself as a cowherd.

Arjuna disguises himself as a eunuch dancing master who wears women's clothing.

Nakula disguises himself as a horse handler.

Book Five: *The Book of the Effort*

At the end of the thirteenth year of exile, when they have not been recognized, the Paṇḍavas demand the return of their kingdom.

Duryodhana refuses to return it.

The Paṇḍavas are supported by seven armies.

The Kauravas are supported by eleven armies.

The Kauravas declare war.

Book Six: *The Book of Bhiṣma*

The eighteen-day battle of Kurukṣetra, involving eighteen armies, begins.

A dejected Arjuna declares his unwillingness to fight and kill his own kin.

Kṛṣṇa, Arjuna's chariot driver, tells him that he must fight and must not fear taking a life that will return.

Kṛṣṇa's words spoken to encourage Arjuna comprise the *Bhagavadgiṭa*, an important Hindu devotional work.

Bhiṣma, the Kaurava general, is mortally wounded, but lives until the battle's end.

Book Seven: *The Book of Droṇa*

Droṇa takes over as commander of the Kauravas.

Abhimanyu, the son of Arjuna and Subhadra, is killed.

Arjuna destroys seven armies.

Droṇa dies in battle, as do Virāṭa and Drupada.

Book Eight: *The Book of Karṇa*

Karṇa takes over Droṇa's position as general of the Kauravas.

Arjuna kills Karṇa in a chariot fight.

Book Nine: *The Book of Śalya*

Śalya, king of the Madras and brother of Gandhari, then becomes general of the Kauravas.

Yudhiṣṭhira kills Śalya.

Bhima kills Duryodhana (crushing his thighs) and Duḥśasana (drinking his blood).

Book Ten: *The Book of the Sleeping Warriors*

Only three warriors of the Kaurava armies remain.

They attack the sleeping warriors of the Paṇḍavas, killing most, including the five sons of Draupadi.

The five sons of Paṇḍu, Kṛṣṇa, and Satyaki, a famed archer, survive.

Book Eleven: *The Book of the Women*

The widows of the fallen warriors grieve.

Dhṛtaraṣṭra orders funeral rites for the fallen.

Book Twelve: *The Book of the Peace*

The dying Bhiṣma instructs Yudhiṣṭhira, despondent because of the great loss of life that has occurred.

Book Thirteen: *The Book of the Instructions*

Bhiṣma's further instructions are presented.

Yudhiṣṭhira is consoled.

Bhiṣma's long life comes to an end.

Book Fourteen: *The Book of the Horse Sacrifice*

Arjuna's grandson, Parikṣit, is born.

Yudhiṣṭhira offers the Aśvamedha.

Arjuna follows and protects the sacrificial horse while it roams the countryside.

Book Fifteen: *The Book of the Sojourn in the Hermitage*

Dhṛtaraṣṭra steps down from his throne.

Dhṛtaraṣṭra, Gandhari, Vidura, and Kunti depart Hastinapura to live the remainder of their lives in the forest.

Book Sixteen: *The Book of the Clubs*

Intoxicated, the warriors of the tribe of Kṛṣṇa annihilate one another in a blood bath.

Arjuna performs the funeral rites of Kṛṣṇa.

Book Seventeen: *The Book of the Great Journey*

Yudhiṣṭhira steps down from the throne, leaving his kingdom to Parikṣit.

Yudhiṣṭhira, his brothers, and Draupadi, accompanied by a dog, set out on a long journey that will mark the end of their earthly lives.

As they eventually approach Mt. Meru, Draupadi, Sahadeva, Nakula, Arjuna, and Bhima, one-by-one, die.

The dog is revealed to be Dharma.

Yudhiṣṭhira ascends to heaven.

Book Eighteen: *The Book of Heaven*

Yudhiṣṭhira, in heaven, is reunited with his family.

3. Primitive Indo-European elements in *The Mahabharata:* the transposition of myth into epic

The tripartition of Indo-European society and the Paṇḍavas (Wikander 1947; Dumézil 1995:95–101)

The "sons" of Paṇḍu are fathered by gods who span the three functions:

- First function
  - Dharma: father of Yudhiṣṭhira
- Second function
  - Vayu: father of Bhima
  - Indra: father of Arjuna
- Third function
  - The Aśvins: fathers of Nakula and Sahadeva

When the Paṇḍavas serve Virata in the thirteenth year of exile, their disguises reflect their tripartite parentage:

- First function
  - Yudhiṣṭhira: disguised as a Brahmin
- Second function
  - Bhima: disguised as a butcher/cook and gladiator-wrestler
  - Arjuna: disguised as a eunuch dance master wearing women's clothing
    - Both the "dance" component and the "elaborate dress" component reflect descriptions of Indra and the Maruts in the Vedic hymns.
    - Compare Heracles and his female dress during his tenure of service to Omphale (Puhvel).
- Third function
  - Nakula: disguised as a horse handler
  - Sahadeva: disguised as a cowherd

Vayu and Indra (Dumézil 1995:92–93; 1992:176–177)

The sons that Vayu and Indra produce for Paṇḍu are reflexes of two different Proto-Indo-European warrior-types, attested in various Indo-European cultures.

Bhima, fathered by Vayu, is typical of the brute, having monstrous strength, whose weapon is commonly his bare hands/arms and, sometimes, a club.

In Greece, Heracles is of the same fundamental type.

Arjuna, fathered by Indra, is typical of the polished and civilized warrior, a master of his weapons.

In Greece, Achilles is of the same fundamental type.

Vayu, a relatively minor deity in the *Rig Veda,* is invoked as one of the two warrior deities who provide sons for Paṇḍu, and, more than that, is called upon before Indra, the greatest of the second function gods.

This tradition of *The Mahabharata* preserves a Proto-Indo-Iranian (thus, pre-Vedic) state of affairs in which Vayu was a deity of elevated significance.

There is other evidence of Indo-Aryan Vayu's earlier importance.

In Iran, the corresponding god Vayu possesses great power.

According to the *Aitareya Brahmaṇa*, when the gods raced, Vayu had first place ahead of Indra, but allowed Indra to finish with him.

Bhiṣma (Dumézil 2000; 1995:210–218; Boyer 1991)

Bhiṣma has a homologue in the Norse god Heimdall.

Bhiṣma is the sky god, Dyaus, in human form.

Heimdall is a god whose dwelling is on Himinbjörg ("Sky Mountain"), next to Bifröst (the rainbow).

Bhiṣma is the first-born of the principal heroes of *The Mahabharata*.

Heimdall is the most ancient of the gods, born at the dawn of time.

Of those heroes who are killed in the battle of Kurukṣetra, Bhiṣma is the last to die.

Heimdall will be the last of the gods to die in the battle of Ragnarök, at the end of time.

Bhiṣma provides for and raises three generations of sons who are not his own.

Heimdall, using the name Rig, mingles among people and engenders three sons for three different couples, keeping his paternal role a secret.

Bhiṣma is one of eight or nine sons borne by the river deity Ganga.

Heimdall is said to have been born from nine sisters ("one and eight mothers"), who are waves of the sea.

Śiśupala: another Indic reflex of the triple-sinning warrior (Dumézil 1983)

At the ceremony honoring Yudhiṣṭhira (Book Two), Kṛṣṇa publicly enumerates five sins committed by Śiśupala.

These sins are clearly distributed across the three functions:

- Śiśupala's first-function sin:

  He stole Vasudeva's sacrificial horse.

- Śiśupala's second-function sins:

  He attacked and burned down the city of the unsuspecting Yadavas.

  He killed and captured unsuspecting rajanyas.

- Śiśupala's third-function sins:

  He twice abducted women belonging to other men.

10 Celtic Society and Religion

Outline of Key Terms and Concepts

1. Identifying the earliest evidence of Celtic culture in Europe is a matter of disagreement.
    - Commonly, the archaeological record of Europe is interpreted as providing such evidence in about 1000 BC.
    - The earliest period of Celtic culture is termed *Halstatt* (after a site in the north of Austria).
        - Halstatt culture spread across Europe beginning in about 800 BC.
    - A second Celtic cultural phase is that of the La Tène period (named for a site in eastern Switzerland), beginning in about 500 BC.
    - The Celts not only moved across most of the European continent, but also pressed into Asia Minor.
    - Scholars debate the date of the arrival of the Celts in the British Isles.
        - Celts had arrived in Britain by the sixth century, perhaps considerably earlier.
2. The earliest Celtic languages attested are varieties of Continental Celtic.
    - Gaulish
        - Gaulish was spoken from Asia Minor west across Europe.
            - Lepontic was spoken in the north of Italy.
            - Galatian was spoken in Asia Minor.
            - Lepontic and Galatian have been called distinct languages, but are probably Gaulish dialects.
        - Gaulish (Lepontic) is first attested in about 600 BC.
    - Hispano-Celtic or Celtiberian
        - Hispano-Celtic was spoken on the Iberian Peninsula.
        - Hispano-Celtic is first attested in about 200 BC.
3. Better attested, but later, are the Celtic languages of Britain and Ireland.
    - Old Irish
        - A few Old Irish inscriptions in the distinctive Celtic script called *Ogham* are attested as early as the fourth century AD.

The majority of Old Irish documents begin to appear only in about the eighth century AD

Old Welsh

Old Welsh is also first attested in about the eighth century AD

4. Within the Indo-European family, Celtic is most closely related to Italic.

   Some scholars have proposed a period of Italo-Celtic linguistic unity, prior to the further development of distinct Italic and Celtic subfamilies.

5. Celtic and Italic languages share certain linguistic features in common with the Indo-Iranian languages.

   In part, this is an expression of the "fringe language" phenomenon.

   Celtic and Italic occur at the western extremity of the area of Indo-European expansion in antiquity.

   Indo-Iranian occurs at the eastern extremity.

   Languages situated on the boundaries of a speech area tend to conserve more inherited linguistic features than languages occurring in the interior of the speech area.

   These unique linguistic similarities, however, are shared lexical items (words) belonging to the semantic realm of religion and law; for example:

   - 'King': Latin *rēx;* Old Irish *rī;* Sanskrit *rāj-*
   - 'I believe': Latin *crēdō;* Old Irish *cretim;* Sanskrit *śraddhā-;* Avestan *zrazdā-*

   The preservation of these words is a consequence of the survival of a powerful priestly element, of common Indo-European origin, in each of these cultures.

   In Celtic society, these priests are the Druids.

6. Celtic society is of tripartite structure.

   In his work entitled *The Gallic War*, Julius Caesar describes the Celtic peoples whom he encountered in Gaul.

   Caesar writes that there are three classes (*genera*) of people (*Gallic War* 6.13–15).

   - Druids: the priests
   - Equites: those who make war

     To name this second class, Caesar adapts a term familiar to him from Roman society.

     In Republican Rome, the Equites ("horsemen") were a group of high economic and social standing, which had provided the cavalry contingent of the Roman military in earlier times.

   - Plebes: the common people, who perform labor and are treated like slaves

In naming the third group, Caesar adapts the Latin term for the class of common people in Roman society.

Old Irish sources attest an equivalent three-class social structure:

- Druid: the priest
- Flaith: the noble; one exercising power
- Bó-aire: the free commoner (literally the 'cattle-commoner', where Old Irish *aire* may be cognate with Sanskrit *ārya-*)

7. In Celtic society, there is a further level of tripartition (Rees and Rees 1989).

   The first function exhibits its own internal three-way division:

   - Druids

     The Druids receive the highest honors in Celtic society.

     They officiate at the sacrificial rites.

     They act as judges.

     They function as teachers.
   - Filid (Old Irish) or Vates (Latin)

     The Filid/Vates practice divination.

     They prophesy regarding future events.
   - Bards

     The Bards compose and sing praise-poetry.

   These three subdivisions can be interpreted as a replication of the three Indo-European functions:

   - Druids: the first function within the first function

     The Druids display both the magical and legal aspects of the inherited Indo-European first function.
   - Filid/Vates: the second function within the first function

     The ecstatic behavior displayed in their prophesying is reminiscent of the Indo-European warrior possessed by warrior madness.
   - Bards: the third function within the first function

     The Bards provide the goods of praise for consumption by the heroes.

8. The earliest sources of information about Celtic religion are the works of Roman and Greek authors.

   Julius Caesar (first century BC), in his *Gallic War* (6.13–16), states that:

   A taboo prevents the Druids from recording their religious knowledge in writing.

   Writing of non-religious documents is, however, permitted.

   Druids serve both as religious leaders and as judges (see above).

   If someone refuses to accept the legal ruling of a Druid, that person is excluded from the sacrificial rites.

Such exclusion results in the person becoming a social outcast.

Within a Celtic community, there is a single chief Druid.

Upon his death, if there is no consensus successor, the Druids elect a new chief Druid.

In some instances, the Druids may resort to armed force to place their candidate in the position of chief Druid.

Druids do not normally serve as combatants in war and are exempt from payment of war tax.

Druidic education consists of committing to memory the vast secret knowledge ("a great many verses") of the Druids.

Druidic training may require up to twenty years.

The central belief of the Druids is that the soul is eternal in nature and transmigrates from one form into another after death.

Druids are students of not only the gods but of nature and astronomy.

Druids sometimes offer human sacrifice, filling wicker figures with victims and setting them ablaze.

There are two reasons for human sacrifice:

- For healing from serious illness
- For protection in battle

Lucan (first century AD), a Roman poet, records in his *Civil War* (1.444–462) that the Druids teach that the soul never enters a netherworld.

It passes from one form of life into another.

Death occurs only in the midst of ongoing life.

The Celtic warrior is thus freed from the fear of death.

It would be cowardly to be protective of a life that will return.

Lucan's description of the Druidic belief and its relevance to the warrior is remarkably similar to Kṛṣṇa's words of encouragement to Arjuna at the outset of the battle of Kurukṣetra (in the *Bhagavadgiṭa*).

Suetonius (first/second centuries AD), the biographer of the Caesars, records (*Claudius* 25.5) that the Roman emperor Claudius banned the practice of Druidism in Gaul (AD 54).

Augustus Caesar had earlier prohibited its practice among Roman citizens.

Tacitus (first/second centuries AD), a Roman historian, records that Druids still remained active in Gaul (in AD 70), prophesying the downfall of Rome (*Histories* 4.54).

Earlier (in AD 61), the Romans had effectively eliminated Druidism in Britain (*Annals* 14.29–30).

The Roman commander in Britain, Suetonius Paulinus, led his troops against Celtic defenders on the Isle of Mona.

The Isle of Mona is modern-day Anglesey.

The island lies just off the northwest coast of Wales.

The Roman infantry crossed to the island by boat.

Celtic defenders stood in battle line on the shore.

Women with disheveled hair, wearing black and carrying torches, ran in and out between the warriors.

Druids stood in a circle with their hands raised, uttering curses against the Romans.

The Roman soldiers were temporarily stunned by the sight.

Upon recovering, they advanced upon and slaughtered the Celts.

The Romans destroyed Druidic groves that stood on the island.

9. Druidism in Ireland

The Romans did not colonize Ireland.

Druidism continued to be practiced until the fifth century AD.

In the fifth century, St. Patrick introduced Christianity to Ireland, abolishing Druidism.

Christian opposition focused on the highest Druid "subclass."

The middle class, that of the Filid, was treated less harshly.

The Filid not only survived as an element of Irish society, but prospered.

The Filid became teachers and royal advisors.

By the thirteenth century, the Filid were also functioning as Bards.

The Filid survived until the establishment of English rule in the seventeenth century.

10. The gods of the Celts

Julius Caesar (*Gallic War* 6.17) identifies the chief deities of Gaul by utilizing Roman divine names.

- Mercury

  The deity most worshipped

  The inventor of all arts

  The guide of roads and journeys

  The god of profit and commerce

- Apollo

  The god who drives away sickness

- Minerva

  The patron deity of arts and skills

- Jupiter
  - The god who holds sovereignty in heaven
- Mars
  - The god who has power over war
    - The spoils and captives of war are offered to him.

Caesar's "Mercury" is probably the god called *Lug* in Ireland.

Lugos or Lugus is his name among Celts of the European continent.

The god's name is preserved in the names of numerous European cities: Lyon, Leiden, Liegnitz, Léon and others, from an earlier Lug(u)dunum.

Lug has the epithet Samildánach ('Possessor of All Arts').

In his description of the Germanic peoples, Tacitus (*Germania* 9.1) names their chief deity also as Mercury.

This "Mercury" is undoubtedly the sovereign Germanic god, Odin or Wodan.

Compare the "translation" of Latin *dies Mercurii* ('the day of Mercury') by Germanic forms such as Old English *Wōdnesdæg* ('the day of Wodan').

Germanic Odin and Celtic Lug bear many similarities (de Vries 1958; 1961).

- Both Lug and Odin are chief of their respective pantheons.
- Both Lug and Odin play a prominent role in a conflict that is crucial for the integrity of their respective societies:
  - In Irish tradition, the Second Battle of Mag Tuired
  - In Norse tradition, the war between the Æsir and the Vanir
    - These are homologous Indo-European traditions.
- Both Lug and Odin fight with a spear.
- Both Lug and Odin are characterized as one-eyed.
- Lug is master of poetic art; Odin is the patron of the skaldic poets.
- Both Lug and Odin are associated with the raven.
- Both can magically affect the outcome of battle.

Tacitus's use of "Mercury" to name Odin lends support to identifying Caesar's "Mercury" as Lug.

If Gaulish "Mercury" is a sovereign deity, then Caesar's Gaulish pantheon conforms to a tripartite structure (de Vries 1961; 1960).

- First function: Mercury and Jupiter (gods of sovereignty)
- Second function: Mars (god of war)
- Third function: Minerva and Apollo (gods of goods production and healing, which is also a third-function activity)

Lucan (*Civil War* 1.444–446) names three Celtic deities to whom human sacrifices are offered:

- Teutates

  A commentary on Lucan (fourth century AD and later) states that Teutates's victims were drowned in a cask.

    Such a sacrifice may be illustrated on the Gundestrup Cauldron (a silver cauldron discovered in a peat bog in Denmark).

  De Vries (1961) proposed that Teutates is to be identified with Lug.

- Esus

  Esus is depicted on the "Paris Altar" (the base of a pillar discovered beneath Notre Dame Cathedral).

    The god is depicted chopping a tree with an ax-like blade.

    On an adjoining side is depicted a bull with three cranes standing on his back and head (*tarvos trigaranus*).

    Dumézil (1942) compared the scene to a variant of the Indic account of Indra's slaying of the Tricephal.

      Indra is assisted by a carpenter.

        The carpenter cuts off each of the three heads of the Tricephal with an ax.

        Out of each neck flies a bird.

    Dumézil thus proposed that, like Indra, Esus is a second-function deity.

  The commentary on Lucan records that Esus's victims were sacrificed by hanging.

    Victims were also sacrificed to Germanic Odin by hanging.

    Because Lug appears to be Odin's Celtic equivalent, perhaps Esus is then to be identified with Lug, a first-function deity (Puhvel).

- Taranis

  The Lucan commentary states that victims offered to Taranis were sacrificed by being burned.

  Taranis's name may be built on the Celtic word for "thunder."

11. The Irish tales

The Irish myths and legends are recorded in various medieval texts.

These texts are grouped into four sets, or cycles.

1. The Mythological Cycle

A large collection of stories concerned chiefly with the Tuatha Dé Danann, the 'People of the goddess Dana'

2. The Ulster Cycle

Also called the "Red Branch Cycle"

A collection of stories concerned with the heroes of the province of the Ulaid (Ulster)

The chief heroes of the Ulster Cycle are Conchobar, the king of the Ulaid, and the greatest of his warriors, Cúchulainn.

Included in the Ulster Cycle is the epic tale of the *Táin Bó Cuailnge* (*The Cattle Raid of Cooley*).

This is the tale of a great conflict between Conchobar and the king and queen of the province of Connacht, Ailill and Medb.

3. The Fenian Cycle

Stories about Fionn mac Cumhaill and his warrior band, the Fianna Éireann

The Fenian Cycle is also called the *Ossianic Cycle*, after the son of Fionn, Oisín.

Many of the stories of the Fenian Cycle center on the provinces of Leinster and Munster.

4. The Historical Cycle or Kings' Cycle

Tales treating numerous Irish kings who lived between the third and seventh centuries AD.

Supplementing the tales of the cycles are other Medieval Irish works.

- The *Dindshenchas (The Lore of Prominent Locales)*

  Various myths and tales of heroes

  Many provide an explanation of topographic names

- The *Cóir Anmann (The Elucidation of Names)*

  Various texts providing explanations of personal names

- The *Lebor Gabála Érenn (The Book of the Conquests of Ireland)*

  A work describing the six successive mythic invasions (settlements) of Ireland

  In the *Lebor Gabála Érenn*, traditional Celtic lore is woven together with Biblical tradition.

12. The invasions of Ireland (*Lebor Gabála Érenn*)

First invasion: led by Cessair, granddaughter of the Biblical Noah

Noah rejects Cessair and her companions as thieves and refuses to allow them to board the ark.

Cessair sails away from her Biblical homeland accompanied by:

Bith: the father of Cessair

Fintan: the husband of Cessair

Map 10–1. Early Ireland

Ladra: the pilot of their ship

A company of forty-nine other women

Cessair and her followers land in Ireland on the coast of Munster.

The fifty women are divided among the three men:

Bith receives seventeen women.

Fintan receives seventeen women, including Cessair.

Ladra receives only sixteen, but soon dies from an overabundance of women.

Bith and Fintan then evenly divide Ladra's sixteen women.

Bith and his twenty-five women companions move northward.

        - Bith dies.
        - The twenty-five women return to Fintan, Cessair, and their companions.
    - Fintan deserts Cessair and the other women.
        - Cessair dies from grief.
        - The remaining women do not survive the coming Flood.
    - Fintan takes refuge in a cave on the Hill of the Wave, where he survives the Great Flood that covers the earth.
    - Fintan is regarded as a great seer in Irish tradition.
        - Fintan has the ability to take on animal shape.
        - Fintan lives for thousands of years, witnessing the ensuing invasions.
- Second invasion: led by Partholón, a descendant of Aithechda, the grandson of Japheth, son of Noah
    - Partholón is a Greek who murders his father, a king.
        - As a consequence, Partholón loses one eye.
    - After wandering, Partholón settles in Ireland with his followers.
        - This second invasion occurs more than 300 years after the first.
    - In Ireland, Partholón and his followers frequently battle the Fomoire.
        - The Fomoire whom they fight came in four ships.
            - Each ship contains fifty male and 150 female Fomoire.
        - The Fomoire are gruesome creatures, having one arm, one leg, and other anatomical abnormalities.
    - Partholón is called the "master of all crafts."
        - Partholón and his followers introduce many crafts, agriculture, and herding to Ireland.
        - They clear four plains and construct seven lakes in Ireland.
    - Partholón's descendants flourish for many years, but then all die from a plague, except for one man, Tuan.
        - Like Fintan, Tuan can take on animal shape.
        - Tuan lives for many years.
        - Eventually, while in the form of a salmon, Tuan is caught.
        - The salmon is eaten by a woman, the wife of Cairill.
        - She then gives birth to Tuan, whose life begins anew.
- Third invasion: led by Nemed, a more distant descendant of Aithechda
    - Nemed is a Scythian.
    - After wandering, Nemed settles in Ireland with his followers.

            - This third invasion occurs 30 years after the demise of Partholón's followers.
        - Nemed defeats the Fomoire in three battles.
        - Nemed's people clear twelve plains and construct four lakes.
        - In a fourth battle, the Fomoire defeat and subjugate Nemed and his followers.
        - Nemed dies of a plague.
        - Nemed's followers attack the Fomoire, but are ultimately defeated.
        - Only thirty of Nemed's followers survive.
        - These flee Ireland in three groups of ten, each led by one of Nemed's sons.
            - One group, led by Fergus Lethderg, flees to Britain.
                - Fergus is ancestor of the British.
                - His descendants play no further role in the mythic invasions of Ireland.
            - A second group, led by Iarbonél the Soothsayer, flees to the far north of Europe.
            - A third group, led by Starn, flees to Greece.
    - Fourth invasion: the coming of the descendants of the Nemedians that had been led away by Starn
        - The Nemedian descendants in Greece become known as the *Fir Bolg*.
            - Old Irish *fir* is the plural of *fer* 'man', cognate with Latin *vir* (as in English *virile*) and Old English *wer* (preserved in English *werewolf* 'man-wolf').
            - The meaning of Old Irish *Bolg* is uncertain.
                - It has been claimed to be from the common noun *bolg* 'bag', with reference to the leather sacks in which the Fir Bolg were required to carry dirt as they labored in Greece.
        - The Fir Bolg come to Ireland many years after the departure of Nemed's sons.
        - The Fir Bolg establish kingship in Ireland and divide Ireland into five provinces.
        - Eochaid mac Eirc, a great king among the Fir Bolg, first establishes justice in Ireland.
    - Fifth invasion: the coming of the descendants of the Nemedians that had been led away by Iarbonél
        - The Nemedian descendants in the far north become known as the *Tuatha Dé Danann* ('People of the Goddess Dana').
            - The mother goddess Dana, or Ana, is the chief goddess of pagan Ireland.
            - Dana appears to have contrastive helpful and harmful aspects.

Dana's Continental Celtic counterpart is **Danu*, as suggested by various geographic names, such as Danube.

In the far north, they acquire Druidic knowledge, great magic, and skill in the arts.

The Tuatha Dé Danann come to Ireland, not by ship, but on dark clouds.

The Tuatha Dé Danann arrive thirty-seven years after the arrival of the Fir Bolg.

They land on a mountain in the province of Connacht.

Their arrival is followed by three days of darkness.

The Tuatha Dé Danann bring with them four talismans:

- The stone of Fál:
  - The stone that identifies the true king
- The spear of Lug:
  - The spear that ensures victory
- The sword of Nuada:
  - The sword from which there is no escape
- The cauldron of the Dagda:
  - The cauldron that always provides food

Dumézil (1992a) has pointed out that traditions of such talismans are found in several Indo-European cultures.

The talismans conform to a tripartite structure:

- First function: the stone of Fál (sovereignty)
- Second function: the spear of Lug and the sword of Nuada (war)
- Third function: the cauldron of the Dagda (provision)

The Tuatha Dé Danann demand that the Fir Bolg give them half of Ireland; their refusal to do so leads to war.

The First Battle of Mag Tuired (*Cath Maige Tuired;* Fraser 1915; Dumézil 1988)

The First Battle of Mag Tuired is fought between the Tuatha Dé Danann and the Fir Bolg for control of Ireland.

The king of the Tuatha Dé Danann is Nuada.

During the battle, Nuada fights with Sreng, a great Fir Bolg warrior.

Sreng severs Nuada's right arm at the shoulder.

At the end of that day, the Tuatha Dé Danann have the upper hand.

In the night, Sreng tells the Fir Bolg that continued battle will bring destruction.

The next morning, Sreng challenges Nuada to personal combat.

Despite his injury Nuada agrees, on the condition that Sreng will tie down his own right arm.

Sreng replies that Nuada's disability places no constraints on the Fir Bolg.

Sreng has a right to resume their personal combat at that point at which they left off the day before.

The Tuatha Dé Danann accede to this right and offer a counterproposal: the Fir Bolg can cease fighting and choose any single province to be their own.

The Fir Bolg accept the offer and choose Connacht.

The First Battle of Mag Tuired ends with sovereignty over Ireland, as a whole, passing to the Tuatha Dé Danann.

Following the battle, the injured Nuada steps down from the throne.

Bres (Eochaid Bres, 'Bres the beautiful') is chosen to be king.

Bres is of mixed heritage.

Bres's father is Elatha, a king of the Fomoire.

Bres's mother is Ériu, one of the Tuatha Dé Danann.

The Tuatha Dé Danann and the Fomoire have become allies.

The Fomoire no longer appear to be the gruesome creatures that they were at an earlier time.

Bres is a cruel and greedy king who oppresses the Tuatha Dé Danann.

Bres demands heavy tribute of the Tuatha Dé Danann and weakens them.

Bres strengthens the kings of the Fomoire.

The Tuatha Dé Danann compel Bres to leave the throne.

Bres assembles a great army of the Fomoire.

Nuada is again chosen to be king of the Tuatha Dé Danann.

Dian Cécht, the great physician among the Tuatha Dé Danann, has made for Nuada an artificial right arm of silver.

Nuada is now known as *Nuada Airgetlám* ('Nuada of the Silver Hand').

After Nuada takes the throne, the Tuatha Dé Danann continue to suffer at the hands of the Fomoire and their great king, Balor.

One day a feast is held at the residence of King Nuada in Tara.

A handsome stranger arrives at the gates of the king.

The stranger identifies himself as Lug Lámfhota ('Lug of the Long Arm').

Like Bres, Lug is of mixed heritage:

Lug's father is Cian, one the Tuatha Dé Danann, the son of Dian Cécht.

Lug's mother is Ethniu, one of the Fomoire, the daughter of Balor.

Lug asks to be admitted to the king's household.

The king's guards (Camall and Gamal) refuse, stating that no one can be admitted except one who possesses some special skill.

Lug states that he is a carpenter, and Camall responds that the king already has a carpenter.

Lug states that he is a smith, and Camall responds that the king already has a smith.

Lug continues to name in turn the skills that he possesses.

Lug claims to be a champion, a harpist, a warrior, a poet, a magician, a physician, a cupbearer, a brass-worker.

Each time, the guard's answer is the same.

Lug then demands to be admitted on the basis that he alone possesses all skills.

He is Lug Samildánach ('Possessor of All Arts').

On this basis, Nuada instructs the guards to admit Lug, who then demonstrates all of these skills to the king.

Nuada gives Lug authority to plan for war with the Fomoire.

Lug deliberates for one year with four other leaders of the Tuatha Dé Danann:

- The Dagda (The 'Good God')

The Dagda is also called *Ruad Rofhessa* ('Lord of Great Knowledge').

The Dagda is the god of Druidism.

- Ogma

Ogma is the great strongman among the Tuatha Dé Danann.

Ogma is credited with inventing the Celtic writing system, Ogham.

Ogma is probably identical to the Gaulish god Ogmios.

The Greek author Lucian (second century AD) describes Ogmios (*Heracles* 1–8):

Ogmios is a Hercules-like figure.

Ogmios is, however, presented as an old man.

Ogmios is a figure of eloquent speech.

- Dian Cécht

Dian Cécht is called "the sage of leechcraft."

Dian Cécht is the god of healing.

Dian Cécht has a son, Miach, who is also a healer, and a daughter, Airmid, who is associated with medicinal herbs.

- Goibniu

  Goibniu is an artisan god.

  Goibniu is the smith among the Tuatha Dé Danann, who provides them with weapons for the war with the Fomoire.

The five Irish gods who take counsel to prepare for war with the Fomoire functionally match the five gods named by Julius Caesar as chief deities of the Gaulish Celts (Dumézil 1992b:150).

- First function

  Ireland: Lug Samildánach and the Dagda

  Gaul: Mercury and Jupiter

- Second function

  Ireland: Ogma

  Gaul: Mars

- Third function

  Ireland: Goibniu and Dian Cécht

  Gaul: Minerva and Apollo

Within a Roman context, the set of gods consisting of Mercury, Jupiter, Mars, Minerva and Apollo has no particular significance.

Within an Irish context, the set of gods consisting of Lug, the Dagda, Ogma, Goibniu, and Dian Cécht has great significance, suggesting that Caesar's Gallic gods are a natural set of Celtic deities.

The Second Battle of Mag Tuired (Stokes 1891; Dumézil 1988)

The Second Battle of Mag Tuired is fought between the Tuatha Dé Danann and the Fomoire for control of Ireland.

Early in the battle, Nuada is killed by Balor.

The Tuatha Dé Danann try to force Lug to remain at the rear; but he escapes and makes his way to the very front of the fighting, emboldening the Tuatha Dé Danann warriors.

At the front, Lug hops on one leg with one eye closed while chanting incantations.

Lug comes face-to-face with Balor, great king of the Fomoire and Lug's own grandfather.

Balor has an evil eye that is only opened during battle.

Four men are required to open the lid covering the evil eye.

The gaze of the eye could devastate an army.

Balor prepares to open the evil eye, but Lug strikes first, hurling a stone or his spear through the eye, which is pushed out the back of Balor's head.

The gaze of the evil eye falls on the Fomoire army behind Balor and devastates it.

Following the battle, the Tuatha Dé Danann capture Bres.

- Bres bargains for his life with offers of agricultural abundance.
  - Bres offers that Irish cattle should always be milk-producing.
    - The offer is rejected.
  - Bres offers that Irish harvests should be abundant.
    - The offer is rejected.
  - Bres offers to tell the Irish when to plough, when to sow, when to reap.
    - The offer is accepted.

The Mórrígan ('Phantom Queen'), the goddess of war-fury, declares the Tuatha Dé Danann victorious.

Badb, another goddess of war and carnage, prophesies of the coming end of the world.

13. Indo-European mythic themes are preserved in the accounts of the Battles of Mag Tuired (Dumézil 1988).

The one-eyed god

- Lug, as he operates on the battlefield of the Second Battle of Mag Tuired, is the Irish reflex of the Indo-European "one-eyed god."
- A homologous figure appears in the mythic history of Rome (Livy 2.9.1–2.10.13).
  - The Tarquins have been driven out of Rome, and Rome is refashioning itself as a Republic (509 BC).
  - Tarquinius Superbus is not, however, ready to cede political control of Rome.
  - The Tarquins recruit the assistance of Lars Porsenna, king of the Etruscan city of Clusium.
  - Lars Porsenna's army launches a surprise attack on the Roman guards posted across the Tiber from Rome.
  - The Roman guards all panic and retreat except for one, Horatius Cocles.
    - Cocles is another of the several Horatii warriors of Rome (Dumézil 1942).
    - Latin *Cocles* means 'one-eyed'.
      - Cocles had lost an eye during previous combat.
  - Cocles exhorts the Romans not to panic, but to destroy the bridge over the Tiber.

- While the bridge is being destroyed, Cocles takes up a position at the head of the bridge, facing the entire Etruscan force.
- The Etruscans are dumbstruck by his audacity.
- The one-eyed warrior casts menacing glances at the Etruscan chiefs and taunts them.
- After hesitating, the Etruscans begin to throw their javelins at Cocles.
- The Etruscans then charge Cocles as the bridge collapses.
- Cocles dives into the Tiber and swims across.

The Roman reflex of the Indo-European one-eyed god is a mortal, Cocles.

- In Rome, inherited Indo-European myth is transposed into historical narrative.

The one-handed god

Nuada, at the First Battle of Mag Tuired, is the Irish reflex of the Indo-European "one-handed god."

A homologous figure again appears in the mythic history of Rome (Livy 2.12.1–2.13.5).

- Lars Porsenna lays siege to Rome.
- A Roman youth, Gaius Mucius, leaves the city and makes his way to the Etruscan camp, intending to assassinate Lars Porsenna.
- Mucius does not recognize Porsenna and kills his secretary instead.
- Mucius is captured and interrogated by Porsenna.
- Mucius tells Porsenna that he is the first of many (300) young Romans who have dedicated themselves to Porsenna's assassination.
- Porsenna orders Mucius to be thrown into the flames unless he reveals the details of the plan.
- Mucius then voluntarily drives his right hand into a nearby sacrificial flame to demonstrate his resolve.
- Lars Porsenna is astounded and orders Mucius to be released.
- Lars Porsenna then makes peace with Rome.
- Mucius will from then on be known as Scaevola ('left-handed').

The Roman reflex of the Indo-European one-handed god is a mortal, Mucius Scaevola.

Celtic-Roman parallels (Dumézil 1988)

In both the Irish Battles of Mag Tuired and Rome's war with Lars Porsenna:

- The reflexes of the Indo-European one-handed god and one-eyed god play a role.

- An oppressive sovereign is overthrown.
  - In Irish tradition, Bres is the oppressor.
    - Bres is forced off the throne, but assembling an army, he continues to pose a threat.
  - In Roman tradition, Tarquinius is the oppressor.
    - Tarquinius is forced off the throne, but assembling an army, he continues to pose a threat.
- A conflict is concluded by exploiting the loss of a right hand/arm.
  - In Irish tradition, Sreng exploits the loss of Nuada's right arm and avoids a Fir Bolg defeat in the First Battle of Mag Tuired.
    - The exploited party (the Tuatha Dé Danann) has the military advantage.
  - In Roman tradition, Mucius exploits the sacrifice of his own right hand and avoids a Roman defeat.
    - The exploited party (Lars Porsenna's Etruscan army) has the military advantage.
  - A reversal:
    - In Irish tradition, it is the opponent of the one-handed figure (one of the Tuatha Dé Danann) who carries out the exploitation.
    - In Roman tradition, it is the one-handed figure (a Roman) himself who carries out the exploitation.
    - But somewhat similarly, in Irish tradition a one-eyed figure appears among both the Tuatha Dé Danann and among their opponents, the Fomoire, as well:
      - Among the Tuatha Dé Danann, it is Lug.
      - Among the Fomoire, it is Balor.
    - In the Roman tradition, the one-eyed figure appears only among the Romans.

The Second Battle of Mag Tuired has been analyzed as the Irish reflex of the Proto-Indo-European tradition of a conflict between the functions (de Vries 1961; Dumézil 1995:317–318).

In the mythic history of Rome, the motif survives in the account of the Sabine War.

Romulus and his Romans represent the functions of sovereignty and warrior might.

The Sabines represent the realm of wealth and fertility.

In the Irish tradition, the leaders of the Tuatha Dé Danann span the three functions, as do the Tuatha Dé Danann generally:

- First function: Lug and the Dagda

- Second function: Ogma
- Third function: Goibniu and Dian Cécht

But the third function represented among the Tuatha Dé Danann entails only the production of material goods and healing.

The fundamental agrarian component of the third function is conspicuously absent.

In the Second Battle of Mag Tuired, it is the Fomoire who represent the third function.

After the battle, Bres (fighting on the side of the Fomoire) bargains for his life with offers of agricultural abundance.

According to the *Lebor Gabála Érenn*, it was the Fomoire who transformed Ireland into a land of sheep (in the time of Nemed).

In the time when the Fomoire persecuted Nemed's followers, the Fomoire demanded from them two-thirds of their grain and milk (agricultural produce) and two-thirds of their children (fertility).

14. The arrival of the ancestors of the Irish: the Sons of Míl or the Milesians (The *Lebor Gabála Érenn* continued)

The Milesians are originally from Scythia.

Míl Espáine is the eponymous hero of the Milesians.

Míl is a descendant of Japheth, Noah's son.

The first leader of the Milesians was Míl's ancestor, Fénius Farsaid.

Also called Fénius the Ancient, Fénius Farsaid was present at the Tower of Babel when the world's languages were differentiated.

Following the instructions of Fénius, his grandson, Goídel Glas, crafted the Irish language out of seventy-two languages.

Míl marries Seang, daughter of the king of Scythia.

Míl and Seang have two sons: Donn and Erech Febria.

After Seang's death, the Milesians move to Egypt.

Míl marries Scota, daughter of the Pharaoh Nectanebus.

Míl and Scota have four sons: Éber, Amairgin, Ír, and Colptha.

Among other important sons of Míl are Éremón and Erannán.

Leaving Egypt, the Milesians wander and arrive eventually in Spain.

In Spain, Míl Espáine dies for unknown reasons.

Íth, one of the Milesians, sees a distant island (Ireland) from a tall tower his people have built.

Caicer, a Druid among the Milesians, had prophesied that the Milesians would be drawn to Ireland after seeing it from a distance and would settle there.

Íth leads an expedition of Milesians to Ireland, where the Tuatha Dé Danann treacherously kill him.

- The Milesians gather a large force and invade Ireland to avenge the death of Íth.
    - Donn is king of the Milesians.
    - Amairgin is a poet and a judge.
    - Éremón is leader of the expedition.
    - Éber will later play a leading role.
    - Erannán and Ír die before the invaders land in Ireland.
- Amairgin is the first to step ashore.
    - Upon landing, Amairgin recites a poem about himself.
        - The poet presents himself as embodying creation.
        - His words closely match words spoken by Kṛṣṇa to Arjuna prior to the battle of Kurukṣetra.
- The Milesians fight and defeat a Tuatha Dé Danann contingent.
- Moving inland, the Milesians meet three goddesses in turn: Banba, Fódla, and Ériu.
- Each goddess tells them that her name is also the name of the island and asks that that name be kept forever.
    - Donn insults Ériu and she foretells his death.
    - Amairgin promises Ériu that the island will continue to have her name.
- Reaching Tara, the Milesians meet the three kings of the Tuatha Dé Danann: Mac Cuill, Mac Cécht, and Mac Gréine.
- The three kings ask the Milesians to leave them in peace for three more days.
- Amairgin agrees, deciding the Milesians will wait in their ships beyond the ninth wave.
- After three days, the Milesians try to return to shore but are continually blown back by a magic wind conjured up by the Druids of the Tuatha Dé Danann.
- Amairgin calms the wind by reciting a poem.
- Donn and Erech Febria drown.
- The Milesians defeat the Tuatha Dé Danann and take control of Ireland.
- Amairgin divides Ireland along a horizontal plane.
    - The portion above ground he gives to the Milesians.
    - The portion below ground he gives to the Tuatha Dé Danann.
        - The Tuatha Dé Danann now become inhabitants of the *śid* mounds.
- With the death of Donn, Éremón and Éber both lay claim to sovereignty.
- Amairgin divides Ireland into a northern and a southern portion.
    - Éremón becomes king of the north.
    - Éber becomes king of the south.
- Éber is dissatisfied with his portion.

Éber attacks Éremón.

Éremón kills Éber and becomes king over both north and south.

In Irish tradition, this was the cause of the long-standing tension between descendants of the two brothers.

Bibliography and Further Reading

Bonnefoy, Yves. 1991. *Mythologies.* Chicago: University of Chicago Press.

Dumézil, Georges. 1995. *Mythe et épopée I. II. III.* Paris: Gallimard.

_____. 1992a. "Les trois fonctions sociales et cosmiques." In *Mythes et dieux des Indo-Européens*, pp. 81–116 [originally published in 1958]. Paris: Flammarion.

_____. 1992b. "Les théologies triparties." In *Mythes et dieux des Indo-Européens*, pp. 117–154 [originally published in 1958]. Paris: Flammarion.

_____. 1988. *Mitra-Varuna.* New York: Zone Books.

_____. 1942. *Horace et les Curiaces.* Paris: Gallimard.

Duval, Paul-Marie. 1991a. "The Religion and Myths of the Continental Celts of Gaul." In Bonnefoy 1991, pp. 242–249.

_____. 1991b. "Esus." In Bonnefoy 1991, pp. 272–273.

_____. 1991c. "Taranis." In Bonnefoy 1991, p. 278.

_____. 1991c. "Teutates." In Bonnefoy 1991, pp. 279–280.

Eska, Joseph. 2004. "Continental Celtic." In Woodard 2004a, pp. 857–880.

Fraser, M. J. 1915. "The First Battle of Moytura." *Ériu* 8:1–63.

Gantz, Jeffrey. 1988. *Early Irish Myths and Sagas.* London: Penguin Books.

Heaney, Marie. 1994. *Over Nine Waves.* London: Faber and Faber.

James, Simon. 1993. *The World of the Celts.* London: Thames and Hudson.

Kinsella, Thomas. 1970. *The Tain.* Oxford: Oxford University Press.

MacCana, Proinsias. 1983. *Celtic Mythology.* New York: Peter Bedrick Books.

MacKillop, James. 1998. *Dictionary of Celtic Mythology.* Oxford: Oxford University Press.

Puhvel, Jaan. 1987. "Celtic Myth." In *Comparative Mythology*, pp. 166–188. Baltimore: Johns Hopkins University Press.

Rees, Alwyn, and Brinley Rees. 1989. *Celtic Heritage.* London: Thames and Hudson.

Rees, Brinley. 1991a. "Druid and Poet: The Irish *Filidh* and the Welsh *Bardd.*" In Bonnefoy 1991, p. 250.

_____. 1991b. "The Mythic Origins and Successive Populations of Ireland." In Bonnefoy 1991, pp. 257–260.

Stokes, W. 1891. "Second Battle of Mag Tured." *Revue Celtique* 12:52–130.

Vries, Jan de. 1961. *Keltische Religion.* Stuttgart: W. Kohlhammer.

_____. 1960. "Die Interpretatio Romana der gallischen Götter." In *Festschrift für Wolfgang Krause*, pp. 204–213. Heidelberg: Indogermanica.

_____. 1958. "L'Aspect magique de la religion celtique." *Ogham* 10:273–284.

Woodard, Roger. 2004a. *The Cambridge Encyclopedia of the World's Ancient Languages.* Cambridge: Cambridge University Press.

_____. 2004b. "Introduction." In Woodard 2004a, pp. 1–18.

11 Scandinavian Myth and Its Indo-European Heritage

Outline of Key Terms and Concepts

1. Indo-Europeans likely inhabited northern Germany and southern Scandinavia by the early third millennium BC.
   - A distinct Germanic linguistic group had evolved by at least 500 BC.
   - From the above areas, Germanic peoples spread both north and south.
     - One of the earliest identifiable Germanic-speaking peoples to leave the ancestral Germanic area were the Goths.
2. Germanic inscriptions are attested as early as about AD 200.
   - The language of the earliest inscriptions is identified as Ancient Nordic.
   - The inscriptions are written in the runic alphabet.
3. The earliest-known Germanic literary work is a Gothic translation of portions of the New Testament.
   - The translation is the work of the Visigothic bishop Wulfila, undertaken in the fourth century AD.
   - Wulfila did not use the runic script for his translation, but developed a distinct Gothic alphabet.
4. The earliest Germanic documents preserving traditions about Germanic deities are Scandinavian works of the thirteenth century AD.
   - Snorri Sturluson: the single most important literary figure of this period
     - Snorri was a native of Iceland, where he served three terms as the presiding officer (the Lawspeaker) of the Althing (the legislative assembly).
     - Snorri authored several works:
       - *Saint Olaf's Saga:* A biographic account of King Olaf the Second (Olaf Haraldsson) of Norway (AD 995–1030)
         - Olaf was chiefly responsible for the Christianization of Norway.
         - Christianity was introduced to Norway and Iceland by Olaf the First (Olaf Tryggvason).
       - *Egils Saga:* A biographic account of Egil Skalla-Grímsson
         - Egil was a tenth-century skaldic poet, mercenary, and farmer.

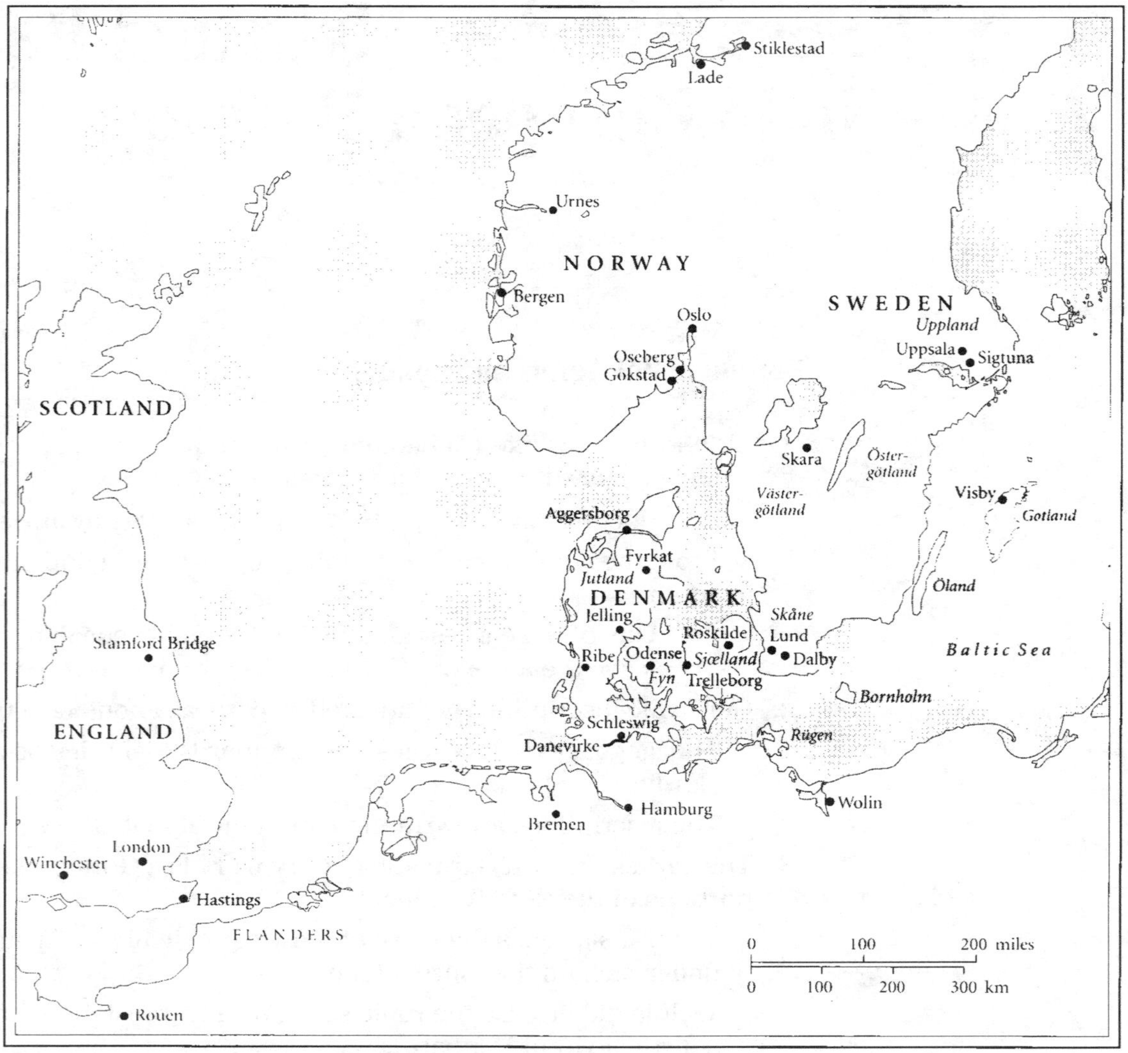

Map 11–1 Viking Age Scandinavia

- The *Heimskringla:* An epic history of the early Norwegian kings
- The *Prose Edda:* A handbook of skaldic poetry

Skaldic verse is the poetic tradition of Medieval Scandinavia, especially associated with Iceland.

Skaldic poetry is technically complex, using a variety of meters, alliteration, internal rhymes, and kennings.

Kennings

Periphrastic metaphorical expressions commonly utilized in early Germanic poetry

Old Norse/Icelandic examples:

Bone-rain for 'blood'

Dwarfs' drink for 'poetry'

Sif's hair for 'gold'

Anglo-Saxon examples:

Whale-pasture for 'sea'

Wave-traveler for 'boat'

Battle-flame for 'sword'

5. Snorri Sturluson's *Prose Edda:* a closer look

Christianity had arrived in Scandinavia only in the tenth century.

During the thirteenth century, there was still a living memory of the pagan traditions.

Though Snorri was a Christian, he believed there was literary value in the old traditions.

To preserve those traditions, he produced his *Prose Edda.*

The meaning of the term *Edda* is uncertain; it may be derived from the Old Norse word *ódr* 'poetry'.

The *Prose Edda* consists of four sections:

1. *Prologue*

This first section of the *Prose Edda* presents a historicized account of the origin of the Norse deities.

The gods are presented as descendants of Trojans who left Asia Minor and migrated to northern Europe.

Snorri thus interprets the Norse gods called the Æsir as "men of Asia."

The Norse gods belong to two groups: the Æsir and the Vanir.

2. *Gylfaginning* (*Tricking of Gylfi*)

The *Gylfaginning* provides a summary of Norse mythic traditions.

Snorri presents these traditions in the form of a dialogue between Gylfi, an ancient king of Sweden, and three mysterious individuals with knowledge of the gods.

Gylfi travels to Asgard, home of the Æsir.

3. *Skáldskaparmál* (*Poetic Language*)

The *Skáldskaparmál* is chiefly an account of kennings.

Snorri presents this discussion in part as a dialogue between Bragi, god of poetry, and the man named Ægir, one skilled in magic.

Ægir travels to Asgard and is entertained by the Æsir.

4. *Háttatal*, (*Account of Meters*)

The *Háttatal* provides a list and discussion of the many skaldic meters.

6. Other important works preserving Germanic mythic traditions
   - The *Poetic Edda*
     - The *Poetic Edda* is a collection of Eddic poems preserved in the thirteenth-century manuscript called the *Codex Regius.*
       - Two of the most important poems:
         - The *Voluspá* (The *'Sibyl's Prophecy'*):
           - A description of the world's creation and its doom
         - The *Hávamál* (The *'Sayings of the High One'*):
           - A wisdom collection and a catalogue of information about Odin
     - Eddic verse is less complex than skaldic verse; the poets are anonymous.
     - The *Poetic Edda* is also called the *Elder Edda,* while Snorri Sturluson's *Prose Edda* is also called the *Younger Edda.*
       - The relative age of the works, which these titles suggest, may not be accurate.
   - The *Gesta Danorum* (The '*History of the Danes*')
     - The *Gesta Danorum* is a thirteenth-century Latin work by Saxo Grammaticus.
       - Saxo was a Danish cleric trained in Latin literary tradition.
     - The work is the source of the story behind Shakespeare's *Hamlet.*
7. The Norse Theogony
   - Snorri Sturluson's *Prose Edda* and the *Voluspá,* the Eddic poem, preserve a creation account.
     - In the beginning there was only Ginnungagap ('Open Void').
     - Niflheim was made: a place of cold and ice and darkness.
       - In Norse tradition, Niflheim is the land of the dead, ruled by Hel, goddess of the dead.
       - Niflheim is joined to Midgard, the world of humans, by a bridge guarded by a giantess.
       - Midgard is joined to Asgard, home of the gods, by the bridge called Bifröst (the rainbow), guarded by Heimdall.
     - In southern reaches, Muspell came to exist: a place of heat and light.
     - Frost and ice from Niflheim and heat from Muspell meet in Ginnungagap.
     - As the heat begins to melt the ice, two creatures emerge from it:
       - Ymir (or Aurgelmir), the first of the frost giants
       - Audhumla, a cow who provides milk for Ymir
     - As Ymir sleeps, he sweats and two more giants grow beneath his left arm; one of his legs conceives a son by the other leg.

- This leg-born son is Thrudgelmir, a six-headed giant (*Vafthrúdnismál;* an Eddic poem).
- Thrudgelmir produces a son, Bergelmir.
- Audhumla, the cow, feeds on salty blocks of ice.
- As she licks one block, another creature, Buri, emerges from it.
  - On the first day his hair appears.
  - On the second day his head appears.
  - On the third day his entire body is uncovered.
- Buri produces a son Bor.
- Bor marries the giantess Bestla.
- To Bor and Bestla, three sons are born: Odin, Vili, and Ve.
- Odin is said to be "ruler of heaven and earth."
- Odin, Vili, and Ve kill Ymir.
  - There is a great flood from his blood.
  - Of the frost giants, only Bergelmir and his wife survive, by climbing into a boat.
- Odin, Vili, and Ve drag Ymir's body to the middle of Ginnungagap.
  - They dismember his body, and from its parts create the earth, sea, and heavens.
    - This tradition is likely of early Indo-European origin.
    - In India, *Rig Veda* 10.90 (the *Puruṣa-Sukta*) preserves a homologous tradition.
      - There exists a great giant, *Puruṣa*.
      - The gods sacrifice *Puruṣa*, dismember his body, and from its parts they fashion the cosmos.
- Odin, Vili, and Ve find two trees on the seashore, an ash and an elm.
  - From the ash tree they created the first man, Ask.
  - From the elm tree they created the first woman, Embla.

The Norse theogony appears to parallel the Greek *Theogony* and the Hittite kingship-in-heaven myth (Littleton).

- Each tradition is crucially concerned with three generations of beings:
  - Greek: Uranus, Cronus, Zeus
  - Hittite: Anu, Kumarbi, Tesub
  - The Norse theogony agrees, showing two sets of three generations of beings:
    - Frost giants: Ymir, Thrudgelmir, Bergelmir
    - Gods: Buri, Bor, Odin
- In each tradition, bodily dismemberment plays a conspicuous role:
  - Greek: Cronus castrates Uranus.

Hittite: Kumarbi castrates Anu.

Norse: Odin and his brothers dismember Ymir.

In the Greek and Norse traditions, following a conflict in which the recognized ruler of gods prevails, the vanquished opponent is relegated to a subterranean existence:

Greek: Zeus confines the Titans to Tartarus.

Norse: According to the Eddic poem, the *Grimnismál*, Odin banishes the giant Bergelmir to an underground abode.

In the Greek and Norse traditions, the recognized ruler of the gods and his siblings belong to a genus of beings that is fundamentally different from that of the beings that they vanquish:

Greek: Zeus is king of the gods; the gods vanquish the Titans.

Norse: Odin is chief of the gods (Æsir); the gods vanquish the frost giants.

Identifying the Norse Theogony as an inherited Indo-European tradition (rather than a borrowing) is complicated by the late date of its attestation (as discussed in Chapter Five).

8. The Æsir: two groups of gods appear in Norse tradition—the Æsir and the Vanir

Odin

Odin is the chief god of the Germanic pantheon.

In Anglo-Saxon (Old English) his name is *Wodan*.

His day is *Wōdnesdœg* 'Wednesday'.

Odin is a god of wisdom.

Odin acquired his wisdom by the voluntary sacrifice of one of his eyes.

Odin's eye is said to lie in Mimir's well, the Well of Wisdom (*Voluspá*).

Mimir is the guardian of that well and a possessor of great wisdom himself.

Mimir belongs to the race of giants, but is closely affiliated with the Æsir.

The Vanir kill and decapitate Mimir during the war between the Æsir and the Vanir.

Odin preserves the severed head of Mimir with herbs, and he consults with it periodically.

Odin will do so for the last time prior to that battle that brings the destruction of the gods and the world, Ragnarök.

Odin is a god of magic and creator of the runes.

The runes are the symbols of the early Germanic alphabetic writing systems.

In Germanic tradition, such an alphabetic script is called a *futhark*.

The name is derived form the order of the first six symbols of the script: *f - u - th - a - r - k*.

The runes are associated with magic.

That association has perhaps been exaggerated in modern times.

Among early Germanic peoples, runes functioned broadly like the letters of any writing system.

Odin acquired his magic through an act of self-sacrifice.

He hanged himself from a tree and inflicted himself with a spear wound (*Hávamál*).

That tree is called the *Yggdrasil*, the World-Tree.

The Yggdrasil has three roots, which reach deep into the earth:

- One root lies in Niflheim.
- One root lies in Jotunheim.

Mimir's well is below this root.

- One root lies in Asgard.

Its branches reach high into the sky.

The tree is inhabited by many wild beasts, some of which have counterparts in Indic tradition (Dumézil 1973a).

In watery depths at its roots lives Nidhogg, a serpent or dragon.

The tree will survive the doom of Ragnarök.

Odin is associated with the *berserkir:* warriors gone berserk with war-fury.

Odin is himself a god of fury and by his magic plays a conspicuous role in war.

His name comes from Proto-Germanic **wōd-ono-* 'raging'.

Odin can inspire his own warriors with excessive madness.

Proto-Germanic **wōd-ono-* is from the Proto-Indo-European root **wet-* 'to blow, to inspire'.

Proto-Indo-European **wet-* is the source of archaic English *wood* 'insane'; Latin *vātēs* 'prophet' (and, hence, English *vatic*).

Odin can bring debilitating fear to the enemies of his warriors.

The cast of Odin's spear, named Gugnir, over an enemy army determines its fate.

Old Norse *berserkir* means 'covered with bear skin'.

Compare with this the Norse warriors called *úlfhednar*, the 'wolf skins'.

Prior to battle, the *berserkir* would work themselves into a howling frenzy, a process called *berserkgangr* ('going berserk').

According to the *Ynglingasaga*, the *berserkir* possessed superhuman strength and stamina (like bears and bulls), fought without armor (like wolves and dogs), and could not be stopped by weapons of steel.

Like Odin, the *berserkir* are said to be shape-shifters, transforming themselves into bears and wolves.

The shape-shifting warrior is known elsewhere in the Indo-European world and is likely a figure of early Indo-European origin (Dumézil 1970).

Dumézil compares with the *berserkir* the Iranian warrior deity Vərəthragna.

Vərəthragna, unlike other warrior gods, survives the reforms of Zarathuštra.

In *Yašt* 14,Vərəthragna metamorphoses into several forms in sequence: the Wind (compare the prominence of Vayu in Iran), an ox, a horse, a camel, a boar, a young man, a bird of prey, a ram, a goat, and a warrior.

In *Yašt* 10, Vərəthragna takes on the form of a boar and precedes Mithra into combat.

Similar warrior figures survive in Celtic tradition, as in the Welsh *Mabinogi:* a collection of Medieval Welsh tales, divided into four parts or "branches."

The fourth branch is the story of Math son of Mathonwy, ruler of Gwynedd (the North of Wales).

Central to the fourth branch of the *Mabinogi* are the children of Math's sister, Dôn.

Dôn is the Welsh counterpart of the Irish goddess Dana.

The Children of Dôn approximately parallel the chief members of the Irish Tuatha Dé Danann:

- Gwydion: a sorcerer
- Eveidd: an escort of King Math
- Gilfaethwy: also an escort of King Math
- Govannon: a blacksmith
- Amaethon: a ploughman
- Arianrhod: the mother of Lleu, counterpart of Irish Lug

The feet of King Math must be held by a virgin at all times, except during war.

- Gilfaethwy lusts after Math's foot-holder, Goewin.
- Gilfaethwy's brother Gwydion, the sorcerer, causes Math to go to war with a neighboring kingdom so that Gilfaethwy's desires can be fulfilled.
- Gilfaethwy rapes Goewin in Math's absence.
- King Math is also a powerful sorcerer; when he learns of Goewin's violation he marries her and punishes Gilfaethwy and Gwydion by successively transforming them into animals.
  - Math changes Gilfaethwy and Gwydion into a female and male deer (respectively) for one year.
    - They produce a fawn.
    - Math transforms the fawn into a boy, named Hyddwn ('little stag').
  - Math then changes Gilfaethwy and Gwydion into a male and female wild hog (respectively) for one year.
    - They produce a young boar.
    - Math transforms the young boar into a boy, named Hychdwn ('tall piglet').
  - Math then changes Gilfaethwy and Gwydion into a female and male wolf (respectively) for one year.
    - They produce a young wolf.
    - Math transforms the young wolf into a boy, named Bleiddwn ('wolf cub').
- Math then returns Gilfaethwy and Gwydion to their human forms.
- Their three sons become three warriors of preeminence.
- Dumézil points out that it is the sorcerer Gilfaethwy (first function) who is ultimately responsible for the generation of the three animal/warriors, as it was his magic that set events in motion that led to their creation.
  - In Germanic tradition, it is Odin, the magician, who inspires the *berserkir.*

One of the celebrated Norse *berserkir* is the warrior Bjarki of *Hrólfs Saga.*

- Bjarki's father was Björn ('bear'), who was a bear by day and a man by night.
- Bjarki's mother was a woman named Bera ('female bear').

Bjarki was one of the three sons borne by Bera.

Elgr, the eldest son, had the shape of a man from the waist up; below the waist he had the form of an elk.

The second-born had the feet of a dog.

The youngest, Bjarki, was fully man but could metamorphose into a bear.

Of the three, Bjarki is the great warrior.

Dumézil sees in Bjarki a "third brother" figure, corresponding to Roman Horatius and Indic Trita Aptya.

By the twelfth century, the practice of *berserkgangr* was prohibited by the Icelandic law code, the Grágás.

Odin is also associated with a second and fundamentally different type of warrior.

This is the chivalrous Odinic hero.

The chief example in Scandinavian tradition is the dragon-slayer, Sigurd Fafnisbane (*Volsunga Saga; Prose Edda*).

Sigurd slays the dragon Fafnir, who guards a treasure of gold.

The treasure had once belonged to Andvari, a dwarf, but the god Loki took it from him by force.

Andvari placed a curse on the ring Andvaranaut, precious to him, so that destruction would come upon any that possessed it.

Sigurd is now doomed.

Sigurd is to be married to Brynhild, a Valkyrie.

Under a magic spell, however, Sigurd marries the princess Gudrun.

Brynhild engineers the murder of Sigurd, but afterward, in grief, falls upon a sword and is burned upon his funeral pyre.

Sîvrit, later Siegfried, is the name of the hero in the cognate Middle High German tradition, the *Nibelungenlied.*

The *Nibelungenlied* also dates to the thirteenth century AD.

It was chiefly the German version that Richard Wagner followed in composing his operatic cycle, *Der Ring des Nibelungen* ('*The Ring of the Nibelungen*').

Wagner also utilized the Norse tradition and created new elements.

Wagner's *Ring* cycle consists of four works:

- *Das Rheingold* ('*The Rhine Gold*')
- *Die Walküre* ('*The Valkyrie*')

- *Siegfried*
- *Götterdämmerung* (*'Twilight of the Gods'*)

Wagner devoted twenty-six years to writing the *Ring* cycle, dedicating the work to his friend and patron Ludwig II, king of Bavaria.

The full *Ring* cycle was performed for the first time in 1876.

Odin may choose for his warriors to die in battle.

Odin's war dead are collected from the battlefield by the Valkyries.

The Valkyries are maiden warriors who convey the chosen warriors to Valhalla, 'Hall of the Battle Slain,' in Asgard.

In Valhalla, Odin's warriors continually fight, always recovering from their wounds, and feast.

Odin's warriors are being kept ready for Ragnarök.

Tyr

Tyr is a second member of the Æsir.

In Anglo-Saxon (Old English) his name is Tiw.

His day is *Tīwesdæg* 'Tuesday'.

In Norse myth, Tyr is best known for his role in the Fenrir episode, recounted in the *Prose Edda*.

Loki and his wife Angerboda had three children:

Fenrir: a wolf

Jörmungand: a monstrous snake

Hel: goddess of the dead

It was prophesied that Loki's children would be a bane to the gods.

The Æsir capture each of Loki's children.

They will raise Fenrir at their home.

Odin throws the snake into the sea around Midgard.

Odin consigns Hel to Niflheim, where she rules.

The Æsir fear Fenrir when they see how quickly he is growing and decide to bind him with a fetter.

Fenrir is willing to be bound; he believes he can break the fetter and he does.

The gods make a second binding, twice as strong as the first, and persuade Fenrir to be bound with it in order to test his strength.

Fenrir agrees and breaks the fetter.

Deeply concerned, Odin sends a messenger to the world of the dark elves, where some dwarves agree to craft a fetter for the wolf.

The fetter is named Gleipnir.

Gleipnir was crafted from six elements:

- The noise that a cat makes as it moves
- A woman's beard
- A mountain's roots
- A bear's sinews
- A fish's breath
- A bird's spittle

Gleipnir has the appearance of a silk ribbon.

The Æsir try to persuade Fenrir to be bound with Gleipnir as a test of his strength.

Fenrir is suspicious.

The gods assure Fenrir that if he cannot break the fetter they will set him free.

Fenrir agrees to be bound only on the condition that one of the gods will place his hand in Fenrir's mouth as a good-faith pledge.

Tyr places his hand in Fenrir's mouth as the guarantee.

Fenrir is unable to break free and bites off Tyr's hand.

Fenrir is kept chained, awaiting Ragnarök, when he will be freed.

Fenrir will kill Odin at Ragnarök.

Odin's son Vidar will then kill Fenrir.

Tyr appears superficially to be a god of war.

Snorri Sturluson (*Prose Edda*) writes that Tyr has power over the outcome of battle and that it is good for the brave to call upon him.

Tacitus (*Germania*) and other Latin sources use the Roman divine name "Mars" to identify Tyr.

Dumézil and de Vries argue that the evidence taken as a whole reveals that Tyr is a god of law (Dumézil 1973a, 1988; De Vries 1956).

Tacitus portrays the Germanic warriors calling not upon Mars (= Tyr) before going into battle, but upon Hercules.

By Latin "Hercules," Roman sources denote the Germanic god Thor.

In Norse literature, Tyr is never depicted in battle or affiliated with battle.

The expected exception is Ragnarök, where all the gods will fight and die.

Tyr will die from wounds he receives slaying Garm, the hound of Niflheim.

Tyr is affiliated with the Germanic legal assembly, the Thing.

In a Frisian inscription, the god is denoted *Thingsus*.

- Tislund in Demark, a meeting place, bears the name of the god.
- Tuesday (Old English *Tīwesdœg*, Old Norse *Tysdag*), Tyr's day, is *Dingesdach* in Middle Low German and *Dinxendach* in Middle Dutch—the day of the Thing.

As a god of law, Tyr would naturally be drawn into the realm of war in early Germanic society, in which war is a legal phenomenon.

- The time and place of combat can be scheduled.
- Legally binding duels can substitute for a confrontation between armies.
- Kennings typically depict combat as a legal phenomenon.

The role of Tyr as a god of law is consistent with the one incident in which he appears in Norse mythology.

- Tyr offers himself a guarantor of the gods' pledge (and forfeits the guarantee).

Tyr voluntarily forfeits his right hand much as Odin voluntarily sacrifices his eye.

Tyr is the Norse reflex of the Indo-European one-handed god.

- Tyr exploitatively loses a hand to bring peace and safety to his people, paralleling the episodes of Mucius Scaevola in Rome and Nuada Airgetlám in Ireland.

Odin is the Norse reflex of the Indo-European one-eyed god.

- Odin uses his magic and one-eyed grimace to bring paralysis and destruction to an enemy army, reminiscent of Roman one-eyed Cocles paralyzing the Etruscans and Irish one-eyed Lug hopping about, pouring curses on the Fomoire.

Tyr, god of law, and Odin, god of magic, embody the two aspects of the Indo-European first function (Dumézil 1988).

- Tyr and Odin thus correspond to the Indic divine pair Mitra and Varuṇa.

Thor

Thor is a third member of the Æsir.

In Anglo-Saxon (Old English), his name is Thunor.

- His day is *Thunresdœg*, later *Thūrsdœg* 'Thursday'.

Thor is the great strongman among the gods.

- He wears a magic belt and gloves that increase his strength.

Thor rides in a chariot drawn by goats.

Thor's weapon is the hammer Mjollnir.

- Mjollnir is fundamentally thunder, and Proto-Germanic **thunaraz* 'thunder' is the source of the god's name.

With Mjollnir, Thor protects the gods from the giants.

The Eddic poem *Thrymsqvitha* tells the story of the theft and recovery of Mjollnir.

- Mjollnir has gone missing.
- Loki is sent to search for it.
- In the land of the giants, Jotunheim, Loki encounters the giant Thrym.
- Thrym says he has stolen Mjollnir and hidden it deep within the earth.
- Thrym offers to return Mjollnir in exchange for the goddess Freyja, whom he wishes to marry.
  - Freyja is daughter of the god Njord and sister of the god Frey.
  - Freyja is goddess of love and fertility.
  - Freyja rides in a chariot drawn by cats.
- Loki reports the offer to the gods, who are willing to make the trade.
- Freyja refuses.
- Heimdall proposes that the gods dress Thor to look like the goddess Freyja.
- Thor at first objects, but then acquiesces.
- The gods dress Thor in bridal clothing, putting on him linen garments, a belt with many keys, jeweled pins, a bridal headpiece, and Freya's own necklace.
  - Freya's necklace is the Brisingamen.
  - The Brisingamen was made by four dwarves, each of whom Freya had to sleep with.
- Loki disguises himself as Thor's handmaid and drives them to Jotunheim.
- Thrym welcomes the disguised Thor and Loki, and they feast.
- Thor eats an ox, eight salmon, three kegs of mead, and all of the delicate dishes set out for the women.
  - Thrym's suspicions are aroused by "Freya's" appetite.
  - Loki, the trickster, sets Thrym's mind at ease by telling him that Freya has been so eager to come to Jotunheim that she has not eaten for eight days.
- Thrym decides to steal a kiss from "Freya," but jumps the full length of the hall when he sees her terrible fiery eyes beneath her veil.
  - Loki again comes to the rescue, telling Thrym that Freya has been so eager to come to Jotunheim that she has not slept for eight nights.

        - Thrym then commands for Mjollnir to be brought in while the wedding rites are celebrated.
        - Thor grabs the hammer and goes to work slaying giants.
    - Thor and Loki in the *Thrymsqvitha* provide Norse examples of the Indo-European warrior in women's clothing.

9. The Vanir
    - Njord
        - Njord is father of Frey and Freya.
            - The three are the principal members of the Vanir.
        - Tacitus (*Germania* 40) tells of a deity named Nerthus.
            - Though Nerthus is female, while Njord (Old Norse *Njörthr*) is male, the two are almost certainly to be equated.
            - Nerthus is worshipped by Germanic tribes of Denmark.
            - Nerthus is "mother earth."
            - Nerthus has a shrine in a sacred grove on a sea island.
                - There she has a sacred chariot, covered by a robe.
            - When her priest determines the time is right, the "goddess" is conveyed among the people in her chariot drawn by cows.
            - There is much celebrating during the period of her conveyance.
                - All weapons are put away, and this is the only time when peace is known.
            - When her priest deems the period for her public appearance has ended, the chariot and robe are cleansed in a lake and returned to the grove.
        - Like Nerthus, Njord and his children are associated with peace and tranquility.
        - Njord is affiliated with the wind and the sea, and is the helper of mariners and fishermen.
        - Njord has enormous wealth and gives prosperity to those who call on him.
        - Njord's wife is Skadi (who gives her name to Scandinavia).
            - Skadi is daughter of the giant Thjazi.
            - Skadi is a hunter who loves to roam the mountains.
            - Njord loves the sea.
            - When Njord and Skadi married, they agreed they would spend nine nights in the mountains, then nine by the sea.
                - But Njord detested the howling of the mountain wolves.
                - And Skadi complained that the sound of the sea birds kept her awake.

- Njord and Frey: divine "twins"
    - Njord and his son Frey are nearly identical figures.
        - Both are associated with the sea.
            - Frey has a magical ship, Skithblathnir.
        - Both marry the daughter of a giant.
            - Frey's wife is the beautiful Gerd ('Earth'), daughter of Gymir.
        - Both are figures of peace and tranquility.
            - Frey conspicuously lacks a sword.
                - He gave his sword to his servant Skirnir, in return for wooing Gerd on his behalf.
        - Both bestow wealth and fertility.
    - The attributes of Njord and Frey clearly place them in the realm of the Indo-European third function (the realm of wealth and fertility).
        - Their similarities make of them a duo reminiscent of the third-function twins of ancient India, the Aśvins.
            - Especially similar are the affiliations of third-function Njord/Frey and the Aśvins with protection of those at sea.
                - The Aśvins also have a magic boat, and among the most famed of their rescuing activities is the recovery of the drowning Bhujyu.
- Freya
    - Freya's affiliations with fertility and sensuality likewise place her within the third function.

10. The Æsir and the Vanir (Dumézil 1973a)
    - The characteristics and affiliations of the Vanir reveal that as a group they constitute the Norse reflex of the primitive Indo-European gods of the third function.
    - In contrast to the Vanir, the class of Æsir, with prominent members Odin (the sovereign deity and magician) and Thor (the deity of physical force), preserves the Indo-European first and second functions.
    - The gods as a whole (both Æsir and Vanir) are often referred to by the formula "Odin, Thor, Frey" or, less commonly, "Odin, Thor, Frey, Njord."
        - The Norse formulae parallel the common Vedic formula: Mitra-Varuṇa, Indra, Aśvins.
    - There was a time, however, when the Æsir and the Vanir were at war with each other.
        - According to the *Voluspá*, the war of the Æsir and the Vanir was the first war the world had seen.
        - Snorri Sturluson writes of the war in both the *Skáldskaparmál* of the *Prose Edda* and the *Heimskringla*.

In the *Skáldskaparmál,* Snorri mentions the occurrence of the war and describes the truce arrangements that were made.

In the *Heimskringla,* Snorri tells how the Æsir and the Vanir attacked each other's territories, how they grew weary of war, and how a peace was concluded with the exchange of hostages.

Dumézil interprets the war between the Æsir (first/second functions) and the Vanir (third function) as the Norse expression of the Indo-European motif of a conflict between the functions.

A Roman homologue is provided by the war between Romulus and the Sabines.

A Celtic homologue is provided by the Second Battle of Mag Tuired, fought between the Tuatha Dé Danann and the Fomoire.

There is also an Indic homologue: the conflict between Indra and the Aśvins at the time the latter are to be admitted to the society of the gods (*Mahabharata* 3.124–125).

There was a time when the third-function deities, the Aśvins, were held distinct from the other gods.

A seer determined to offer a soma sacrifice to the Aśvins.

The soma sacrifice is one of the most important sacrificial rites of Vedic India.

Soma is a fermented vegetable substance having hallucinogenic properties.

Priests ingest the juice of soma pressings in offering the material to the gods.

The identification of the soma plant is uncertain.

Among ideas proposed is that the soma plant is a mushroom, Amanita muscaria (Wasson).

Indra objected that the Aśvins were but healers and servants of the gods and not worthy of the sacrifice.

The seer persisted, Indra brandished his thunderbolt, and a confrontation followed.

The Norse and Indic traditions of the inter-functional conflict: a further look

The Æsir and the Vanir ratify a truce in the following way (*Prose Edda*).

The Æsir and the Vanir spit into a crock.

From this, the gods fashion a man, Kvasir.

Scholars have noted that the name *Kvasir* is related to Indo-European words denoting intoxicating beverage, for example:

Old Church Slavic *kvasŭ* 'bitter drink' and Russian *kvas* 'bitter beer'

These and related words developed from Proto-Indo-European **kwat-* 'to ferment'.

- The use of spittle as a catalyst in the fermentation of fruits is well known.

Kvasir is a man famed for his extraordinary wisdom.

One day at a feast, two dwarves kill Kvasir.

The dwarves drain his blood into two crocks and a kettle.

With his blood, the Dwarves mix honey and create a mead (an intoxicating beverage).

- Whoever drinks this mead becomes a poet.

The dwarves cover up their violent deed by telling the Æsir that Kvasir had choked on the great knowledge that had welled up within him.

In the Indic tradition, the inter-functional conflict will be peacefully resolved after the seer reacts, seeing Indra threatening to use his thunderbolt.

The seer is Cyvana, a powerful ascetic.

- Cyvana intends to offer the soma sacrifice to the Aśvins because they have restored his youth.

As Indra throws his thunderbolt, Cyvana paralyzes Indra's arm.

With his great *tapas*, Cyvana creates a gigantic monster, Mada.

- *Mada* means 'drunkenness'.
- His gaping mouth stretches from earth to heaven.
- His fangs are many miles in length.

Mada attacks Indra.

Indra panics and proclaims that the Aśvins will henceforth be worthy of the soma offering.

- With this concession the Aśvins are said now to have joined the gods.

Cyavana then takes his monster Mada and divides his body into four "intoxicating" constituents: liquor, women, gambling, and hunting.

Dumézil (1986; 1973a) argues that the Norse and Indic inter-functional conflict myths show certain particular and original similarities.

At the point in time when the deities of sovereignty and physical force and the deities of fecundity are socially united in peace, there is created a being that:

- Embodies the power of intoxication
- Bears a name affiliated with intoxication

That being is an excessive force.

- The excess is positive in the Norse tradition of Kvasir.
- The excess is negative in the Indic tradition of Mada.

As a consequence of the being's excessiveness, it is destroyed and divided into intoxicating components.

- The components are presented as beneficial in the Norse tradition.
- The components are presented as harmful in the Indic tradition.

Dumézil offers an interpretation of the origin of the prototype of these motifs among primitive Indo-European peoples.

- Intoxicating substances were consumed to enhance the performance of both sorcerer-magicians and hunter-warriors (demand).
- The growth of plants required for manufacturing such intoxicating substances was controlled within the domain of farmers (supply).
- "Intoxication" is thus portrayed as coming into being at that moment when priests (first function) and warriors (second function) were "reconciled" with agriculturalists (third function)—that is, when society was fully formed.

Dumézil (1996; 1973a; 1973b) argues for an additional homologous feature—a complex feature of two parts, shared by the Norse and Roman inter-functional conflict myths.

In the war between Romulus and his warriors (first/second function) and the Sabines (third function), the Sabine army is aided in its assault on Rome by the traitor Tarpeia, daughter of the commander of the Roman forces on the Capitoline Hill.

- Gold-lusting Tarpeia bargains to allow the Sabine army to enter the Capitoline walls in exchange for their jewelry.
  - A female figure similarly plays a conspicuous role in the Norse tradition of the war between the Æsir and the Vanir.
    - The Eddic poem *Voluspá* (stanzas 21–22) relates how a woman of the Vanir (third function) comes among the Æsir (first/second function).
    - The woman's name is Gullveig, which means 'Madness of Gold' or 'Power of Gold'.
    - Gullveig is a sorceress who attempts to control the Æsir.
    - The Æsir pierce her with their spears and burn her three times in Odin's hall, though she continues to live.

In the Roman account, following the treachery of Tarpeia, the Sabines and Romans meet in open battle.

- A Sabine rout of the Romans is halted when Romulus calls upon Jupiter (first-function deity), who magically intervenes on behalf of the Romans, though the intervention does not eventuate in a military victory for Rome.
  - In the Norse account, following the Gullveig episode, the bulwark of the Æsir collapses, the Vanir and Æsir

meet in battle, and Odin (first-function deity) makes his spear toss into the ranks of the Vanir.

While Odin's spear toss customarily brings destruction to an enemy host, it does not give the Æsir a military victory in this, the first war of the world.

The Roman and Norse accounts of the inter-functional conflict preserve an idiosyncratic complex of events that must have their origin in a common ancestral myth.

A feminine figure notionally associated with gold surreptitiously intervenes on the side of the representatives of wealth and fecundity.

Her intervention weakens the representatives of sovereignty and physical force who counter by the magic intervention of the sovereign god.

The sovereign god's intervention does not bring military victory to the representatives of sovereignty and physical force.

Instead, a treaty is concluded that results in a fusing of the warring sides into a single society.

Bibliography and Further Reading

Chickering, Howell. 1989. *Beowulf.* New York: Anchor Books.

Davidson, Hilda, and Peter Fisher. 1996. *Saxo Grammaticus: The History of the Danes.* Cambridge: Brewer.

Dumézil, Georges. 2000. *Mythes et dieux de la Scandinavie ancienne.* Paris: Gallimard.

_____. 1996. *Archaic Roman Religion.* Reprint edition. Baltimore: Johns Hopkins University Press.

_____. 1988. *Mitra-Varuna.* New York: Zone Books.

_____. 1986. *Loki.* Paris: Flammarion.

_____. 1973a. *Gods of the Ancient Northmen.* Berkeley and Los Angeles: University of California Press.

_____. 1973b. *From Myth to Fiction.* Chicago: University of Chicago Press.

_____. 1970. *The Destiny of the Warrior.* Chicago: University of Chicago Press.

Faarlund, Jan Terje. 2004. "Ancient Nordic." In Woodard 2004, pp. 907–921.

Gantz, Jeffery. 1976. *The Mabinogion.* New York: Dorset Press.

Gentry, Francis et al. 2002. *The Nibelungen Tradition.* London: Routledge.

Haywood, John. 2000. *Encyclopaedia of the Viking Age.* London: Thames and Hudson.

Hreinsson, Vidar. 1997. *The Complete Sagas of the Icelanders.* Reykjavik: Leifur Eiriksson Publishing.

Jasanoff, Jay. 2004. "Gothic." In Woodard 2004, pp. 881–906.

Littleton, Scott. 1970. "The 'Kingship in Heaven' Theme." In *Myth and Law Among the Indo-Europeans*, pp. 83–121. Edited by J. Puhvel. Los Angeles: The University of California Press.

MacKillop, James. 1998. *Dictionary of Celtic Mythology.* Oxford: Oxford University Press.

Page, R. I. 1987. *Runes.* Berkeley and Los Angeles: University of California Press.

Puhvel, Jaan. 1987. "Germanic Myth." In *Comparative Mythology*, pp. 189–221. Baltimore: Johns Hopkins University Press.

Sawyer, Peter. 1997. *The Oxford Illustrated History of the Vikings.* Oxford: Oxford University Press.

Terry, Patricia. 1986. *Poems of the Vikings.* London: Macmillan Publishing.

Vries, Jan de. 1956. *Altgermanische Religionsgeschichte.* Berlin: de Gruyter.

Wasson, Gordon. 1968. *Soma: Divine Mushroom of Immortality.* New York: Harcourt Brace Jovanovich.

Woodard, Roger. 2004. *The Cambridge Encyclopedia of the World's Ancient Languages.* Cambridge: Cambridge University Press.

Young, Jean. 1954. *The Prose Edda of Snorri Sturluson.* Los Angeles and Berkeley: The University of California Press.

Practice Exams

Practice Exam 1–1

Choose the most correct answer from the list at the bottom of the page and write that answer in the space at the end of the question. A single answer can be used only once. Not every possible answer will be used.

1. A Baltic language of the Indo-European language family: ____________
2. Founder of the modern study of general linguistics: ________________
3. Vladimir Propp belonged to the early school of structuralism called __________________.
4. This king called upon Jupiter Stator in a desperate moment: __________________
5. The Flamen Dialis was not allowed to look at __________________.
6. Dumézil argued that this deity belongs to that group called the "first gods": __________________
7. This priest supervised the Vestals: __________________
8. The Greek author Pausanias wrote that Zeus, Hera, and Athena were worshipped together in the Greek city of __________________.
9. Last Etruscan king of Rome: __________________
10. Foster mother of Romulus and Remus: __________________
11. At the Summer Consualia, Consus was worshipped at an altar located within the __________________.
12. An Indo-European subfamily that consists of only a single language: __________________
13. These household gods were said to have been brought by Aeneas: __________________
14. Possible homeland of the original Indo-European community: __________________

Answers: *Lares, his wife, Forum, Janus, Flamen Dialis, Athens, Ferdinand de Saussure, Acca Larentia, Vesta, Armenian, Romulus, Tullus Hostilius, Prague School Structuralism, Penates, Finnish, Phocis, Avestan, Rhea, Robigalia, Circus Maximus, Pontifex Maximus, Tarquinius Superbus, Lithuanian, China, the Pontic Steppe, Russian Formalism, the army, Ancus Marcius*

Exam 1–1, page 2

1. God of wisdom who helped Tesub defeat his final enemy: ___________________

2. Jupiter caused the ancile to fall from heaven into Rome during the reign of ___________________.

3. According to Hesiod, in the beginning there was ___________________.

4. Author of the *Bibliotheca:* ___________________

5. Hittite Ullikummi corresponds to Greek ___________________.

6. The Greek goddess Aphrodite may have her origin in the Phoenician goddess ___________________.

7. The fire that burns in Vesta's temple must be generated from this: ___________________

8. King of Alba Longa who set Romulus and Remus adrift in the Tiber River: ___________________

9. According to Dumézil, in the mythic history of Rome the Sabines represent which of the Indo-European functions? ___________________

10. This warrior killed both a triple enemy and his sister: _______________

11. He swallowed each of his children as they were born: _______________

12. The priest who is said to have taken over the religious duties of the Roman king: ___________________

13. A wife of Zeus who was one of the daughters of Oceanus and Tethys: ___________________

14. Romulus was said to have been transformed into this god: __________

15. Possible destroyers of both the Mycenaean and Hittite civilizations: ___________________

Answers: *Mnemosyne, Ea, arbor felix, second, Cronus, Chaos, Cybele, Numa Pompilius, Tartarus, Tarpeia, Anu, Amulius, Rex Sacrorum, Janus, Numitor, Quirinus, Zeus, Metis, Hurrians, pine cones, Mars, Typhoeus, Apollodorus, Ovid, Sea Peoples, third, Astarte, Flamen Dialis, Horatius, Tullus Hostilius, Plato*

Exam 1–1, page 3

1. Mother of the Graces: ___________________

2. Syllabic script of the Mycenaean Greeks: ___________________

3. Feast of Fornax held on the day of the Quirinalia: ___________________

4. Spirits who avenge crimes; offspring of Gaea: ___________________

5. Pre-Greek civilization of Crete: ___________________

6. Babylonian version of the kingship-in-heaven myth:

   ____

7. Leader of the Sabines; he became co-regent with Romulus:

   ____

8. Romulus watched for birds on the Palatine; Remus watched on the

   ___________________.

9. Mother of Apollo and Artemis: ___________________

10. Lévi-Strauss illustrated his methodology by analyzing the myth of

    ___________________.

11. Cronus was released from captivity to become king of the

    ___________________.

12. Aphrodite was his mother; Ascanius was his son: ___________________

13. A member of both the Pre-Capitoline and Capitoline triad:

    ____

14. Place where Vestals were entombed alive for the loss of virginity:

    ____

15. Daughter of the Titans Hyperion and Theia: ___________________

Answers: *Aeneas, Hera, Minoan, Larentalia, Hittite, Oedipus, Meliae, Jupiter, Shāhnāmeh, alphabet, Selene, Anchises, Eurynome, Erinyes, Mars, Mettius Fuffetius, Jason, Capitoline, Aventine, Leto, Linear B, Circus Maximus, Titus Tatius, Elysian Islands, Campus sceleratus, Cyclades, Stultorum feriae, Enuma Elish, Demeter*

Practice Exam 1–2

Choose the most correct answer from the list at the bottom of the page and write that answer in the space at the end of the question. A single answer can be used only once. Not every possible answer will be used.

1. An Anatolian language of the Indo-European language family: ________________

2. French structuralist who gave us the mytheme: ________________

3. Propp said that all "folk tales" consist of a sequence of ________________.

4. The priest who took over the religious duties of the king: ________________

5. The Flamen Dialis was prohibited from saying the Latin word for ________________.

6. The Brahmins of India were prohibited from having contact with smoke from a ________________.

7/8. The Pre-Capitoline Triad consisted of Jupiter, ________________, and ________________.

9. First Etruscan king of Rome: ________________

10. Festival dedicated to the spirit of wheat rust: ________________

11. One of the subdivisions of the Celtic language group: ________________

12. Roman household gods that were worshipped at crossroads: ________________

13. The Roman god of stored grain: ________________

14. Ancus Marcius built the ________________.

Answers: *Minerva, Dumézil, Lares, hearth, Mars, functions, Hittite, Ceres, Goidelic, Egypt, dog, Pontifex Maximus, Robigalia, Juno, Sabellian, Fornacalia, Pons Sublicius, Consus, Penates, funeral pyre, Rex Sacrorum, Lévi-Strauss, the Pontic Steppe, tower of Pisa, Quirinus, Tarquinius Priscus, Russian, wine*

Exam 1–2, page 2

1/2. The two aspects of the Indo-European first function: ________________ and ________________.

3. The dancing priests of Mars: ________________

4. The son of Iapetus who gives fire to humans: ________________

5. Mother of Uranus: ________________

6. The gods used this weapon to defeat Ullikummi: ________________

7. Youngest of the Titans; he overthrew his father: ________________

8. Name that scholars give to the syllabic script of the Mycenaeans: ________________

9. One of the "divine twins" of the Roman mythic history: ________________

10. Sons of Gaea and Uranus who have one eye each: ________________

11. The first wife of Zeus, according to Hesiod: ________________

12. The ancile fell to earth during the reign of ________________.

13. The Flamen Dialis cannot ride a ________________.

14. The father of modern general linguistics: ________________

15. Founder of the town of Alba Longa: ________________

Answers: *Salii, Latinus, Linear B, Tullus Hostilius, Prometheus, distant, Zeus, Romulus, Cronus, Gaea, horse, Leto, spear, Flamen Martialis, Ascanius, Chomsky, Hecatoncheires, copper cutting tool, Numa, near, Saussure, Cyclopes, magical, Horatius, Metis, legal, Alfred Lobel, elephant*

Exam 1–2, page 3

1. Hurrian storm god: ___________________

2. Titan whose son is the sun: ___________________

3. Greek goddess not found in Mycenaean tablets: ___________________

4. Shepherd who raised Romulus and Remus: ___________________

5. A form of the kingship-in-heaven myth is attested among these Indo-European people: ___________________

6. Dumézil says they represent the third function in the mythic history of Rome: ___________________

7. The destruction of the Mycenaean and Hittite civilizations may have been caused by ___________________.

8. Related words in sister languages that develop from a single word in the common parent language: ___________________

9. A Roman god of beginnings: ___________________

10. Dumézil argues that Quirinus was the Roman god of _______________.

11. The goat who nursed baby Zeus: ___________________

12. Festival at which the Flamen Martialis probably presided: ___________________

13. Goddess who saved Tullus Hostilius: ___________________

14. Romulus was said to have been changed into this god at the end of his life: ___________________

15. First king of Rome: ___________________

Answers: *Tesub, Aphrodite, homologues, Vesta, Sabines, Enlil, Curiatii, Hyperion, Minerva, Assyrians, fire, cognates, Janus, Athena, Norse, grain, Acca Larentia, Quirinus, tidal waves, Romulus, Saturnus, Atlas, Albans, Amalthea, Faustulus, Oceanus, Sea Peoples, Equus October, Robigalia, Ops, Tarquinius Priscus*

Practice Exam 2–1

Choose the most correct answer from the list at the bottom of the page and write that answer in the space at the end of the question. A single answer can be used only once. Not every possible answer will be used.

1. Callisto was what kind of nymph? ____________
2. One of the three Fates—the one who spins the thread: ____________
3. Heracles was dressed as a woman while he served as the slave of ____________.
4. A nymph of springs and other flowing waters is called a ____________.
5. A Thracian earth goddess in origin; the Greeks identified her as the mother of Dionysus: ____________
6. Wife of Heracles; sister of Meleager; tricked by Nessus: ____________
7. Daughter of Zeus and Demeter who was abducted by Hades: ____________
8. Daughter of Agenor whom Zeus abducted in bull-form: ____________
9. Apollo's epithet (title) that is derived from the Greek word for mouse: ____________
10. The mother of Heracles: ____________
11. Paris judged a beauty contest between Hera, Aphrodite, and ____________.
12. Some scholars claim that we can see a Greek survival of Proto-Indo-European tripartite ideology in the story of the ____________.
13. The three-headed hound of Hades: ____________

14. Heracles used this monster's blood to poison his arrows:

____

15. The head of the Equus October is fought over by residents of the Sacra Via and residents of the __________________.

16. The Aśvamedha makes clear that the Equus October is a sacrifice made on behalf of the __________________.

Answers: *Lydia, Lachesis, Dryad, Megara, Pluto, Subura, Deianira, Persephone, king, Athena, flaying of Marsyas, Lernaean Hydra, Smintheus, Artemis, Cybele, shield of Achilles, Clotho, Naiad, Typhoeus, Europa, grain crop, Oread, Alcmena, Tellus, Cerberus, Omphale, Semele, Leto, Eurystheus, Metis, Mnemosyne*

Exam 2–1, page 2

1. Young Hermes stole cattle from ________________.
2. Vedic god who represents the legal aspect of the first function: ________________
3. The elite warrior group of Mitanni: ________________
4. The triple-sinning warrior in ancient India: ________________
5. Indo-Aryan god who shares several characteristics with Greek Hermes: ________________
6. A Thracian king who persecuted Dionysus and died hated by all the gods: ________________
7. Ixion's offspring by the cloud-clone: ________________
8. Artemis is affiliated with both the hunt and with ________________.
9. Like Indra, this Roman warrior was saved by the intervention of three third-function deities: ________________
10. The Indo-Aryan rain god finds a cognate deity in Lithuanian ________________.
11. Heracles cleaned out the stables of ________________.
12. Marsyas was one of those creatures called a ________________.
13. Meleager chose to give the boar's hide to this woman warrior: ________________
14. Rudra is the predecessor of this important Hindu god: ________________
15. Heracles' third-function sin involved the abduction of ________________.
16. The Indic goddess of prosperity: ________________
17. The color worn by priests in ancient Iran: ________________

Answers: *Mitra, Lycurgus, grape-picking, Perkunas, Persephone, Athena, Pentheus, red, Iole, Indra, Idas and Lynceus, nymph, white, Apam Napat, Gandharvas, Śri, childbirth, Vayu, satyr, Dakṣa, Atalanta, Puṣan, Horatius, Viṣṇu, Geryon, Maryanni, Centaurus, Tullus Hostilius, Augeas, Manu, Apollo, Śiva*

Exam 2–1, page 3

1. The Dioscuri and the Aśvins are both affiliated with ______________.
2. A trifunctional deity of Vedic India: ________________
3. Nymph-like, female figures in Indic tradition: ________________
4. Queen of the Amazons whose belt Heracles was sent to fetch: ________________
5. The general name denoting the third-function element of divine society in Vedic India: ________________
6. Son of Zeus and Europa who becomes a judge of the dead: ________________
7. Indra's "triple enemy" executed by Trita Aptya: ________________
8. According to Dumézil, Trita Aptya finds a counterpart in Roman ________________.
9. One of the old sea gods of the Greeks, he is a shape-shifter and has all knowledge: ________________
10. Associated with Mitra, he sees that society's goods are rightly distributed: ________________
11. Sumakhas is to one of the "sons of Dyaus" as ________________ is to one of the Dioscuri ("the sons of Zeus").
12. Husband of Aphrodite and brother of one of her lovers: ______________
13. Gods of the storm winds; Indra said they deserted him in his fight with the dragon: ________________
14. Eurystheus sent Heracles to Crete to bring back the ________________ of Minos.
15. Each of these gods has a rodent affiliation: Rudra, Gaṇeśa, Apollo, and ________________.
16. A Brahmin who castrates Indra with a curse: ________________
17. Old Norse thunder deity who is likely related to Indic Parjanya: ________________

Answers: *Hippolyta, Niobe, hound, Sarpedon, Bhima, Fjörgyn(n), Tyndareus, Namuci, Gautama, Hephaestus, Gandharvas, Adityas, Medea, Asclepius, mariners, Leucippus, Vayu, Horatia, Rhadamanthys, Triśiras, Odin, amphibians, bull, Neptune, Mars, Proteus, boar, Apsaras, Agni, Maruts, Horatius, Vasus, Bhaga, Viṣṇu, Rudras*

Practice Exam 2–2

Choose the most correct answer from the list at the bottom of the page and write that answer in the space at the end of the question. A single answer can be used only once. Not every possible answer will be used.

1. Actaeon was turned into a deer by __________________.
2. Achilles hid among the daughters of the king of Scyros, but was discovered by __________________.
3. After he killed the warrior Iphitus, Heracles became a slave to __________________.
4. The nymphs of the mountains are called __________________.
5. This god was rescued from his mother's ashes: __________________
6. The golden apples of the Hesperides were stolen by __________________.
7. The Centaur killed by Heracles: __________________
8. A king who was killed by his own mother: __________________
9. Hera transformed her into a bear: __________________
10. The "twin" brother of Heracles: __________________
11. The two-headed hound killed by Heracles: __________________
12. The three-bodied giant whose cattle Heracles stole: __________________
13. The three old women who control a person's destiny: __________________
14. A swamp serpent killed by Heracles with the aid of Iolaus: __________________
15. Wife of Tarquinius Collatinus who was violated by Sextus: __________________
16. The __________________ *Veda* was named for the first fire priest.

Answers: *Athena, Artemis, Arachne, Dionysus, Orthus, Europa, Heracles, Iphicles, Apollo, Hydra, Amphitryon, Dryads, Atharva, Iole, Eurystheus, Lucretia, Typhoeus, Odysseus, Cerberus, Pentheus, Lycurgus, Nessus, Omphale, Yajur, the Fates, Augeas, Geryon, Callisto, the Hesperides, the Muses, Oreads, Echidna*

Exam 2–2, page 2

1. Son of Hermes and Aphrodite: ___________________

2. These divine warriors are Rudra's sons and Indra's companions:

   ____

3. This Greek seer healed the daughters of Proetus of their madness:

   ____

4. Mortal woman who challenged Athena to a weaving contest:

   ____

5. After he ascends to Mt. Olympus, Heracles takes this goddess as his wife: ___________________

6. Indra killed this former enemy with the foam of a wave:

   ____

7. The probable Roman homologue (counterpart) of the former enemy killed by Indra: ___________________

8. Leader of the Greek expedition to Troy; he sacrificed his daughter:

   ____

9. Like Vivasvat, Ixion had intercourse with the ___________________ of a goddess.

10. The sister of Semele whom Hera persecuted for taking care of young Dionysus: ___________________

11. Indo-Aryan god representing the magical aspect of the first function:

    ____

12. The Indo-Aryan gods of the third function are called the

    ___________________.

13. The earliest evidence of an Indo-Iranian language comes from

    ___________________.

14. The birds that Heracles got rid of: ___________________

15. The "three-stepping" Vedic god who creates and maintains space:

    ____

16. The victim of both the Aśvamedha and the Equus October is chosen by a ____________________

17. Greek *kentauros* and Sanskrit ____________________ are phonetically and semantically similar, but are not cognates.

Answers: *Hermaphroditus, Melampus, gandharvas, Menelaus, Iphitus, Mettius Fuffetius, Calchas, chariot race, Tullus Hostilius, Cadmus, Lydia, Maryanni, Maruts, Adonis, žindūrv, Mitanni, Mitra, Stymphalian, Ino, clone, Hestia, Erymanthian, Agamemnon, casting of lots, Arachne, Namuci, Vasus, Viṣṇu, friend, Varuṇa, Hebe, Curiatii*

Exam 2–2, page 3

1. Rod carried by the devotees of Bacchus: ___________________

2. The Dioscuri and the Aśvins are both said to be sons of the ___________________.

3. "Twin" brother of Heracles: ___________________

4. The offspring of Vivasvat and Savarṇa; a new kind of creature in the world: ___________________

5. This god was thrown off of Olympus and rescued by Thetis: ___________________

6. Satyr killed by Apollo for losing a musical contest: ___________________

7. Poseidon is god of the sea, god of earthquakes, and god of ___________________.

8. These Greek "boys" alternate between being in the world of the dead and the world of the living: ___________________

9. Indra's great deed was the destruction of this cattle-thieving, drought-bringing monster: ___________________

10. Zeus prevented Arcas from spearing his mother, the bear, by turning them both into ___________________.

11. Like Greek Apollo, this god of India is both healer and destroyer: ___________________

12. For killing Poseidon's son, this god had to become the slave of a mortal: ___________________

13. According to Dumézil, this god is an Indic reflex of the triple-sinning warrior: ___________________

14. To steal the apples of the Hesperides, the thief enlisted the aid of ___________________.

15. Third-function goddess who helped Indra (as Ops had helped Tullus Hostilius): ___________________

16. To cause the winds to blow, Agamemnon sacrificed ___________________, his daughter.

17. He is the fire within the waters and at least of Proto-Indo-Iranian origin: ___________________

Answers: *Dioscuri, Apam Napat, Iolaus, Saraṇyu, Ares, thunder, Iphigenia, Drago, Clytemnestra, Hermes, Indra, sun, Manu, Atreids, Iphicles, constellations, Helios, Gandharvas, Midas, Mitra, Menaka, Hephaestus, horses, Atlas, Vṛtra, sky god, Rudra, Sarasvati, birds, Marsyas, thyrsus*

Practice Exam 3–1

Choose the most correct answer from the list at the bottom of the page and write that answer in the space at the end of the question. A single answer can be used only once. Not every possible answer will be used.

1. Credited with inventing the Celtic writing system: ________________
2. He banished the practice of Druidism in Ireland: ________________
3. Leader of the second wave of invaders to settle Ireland: ________________
4. The final battle between the Paṇḍavas and the Kauravas: ________________
5. Norse reflex of the Proto-Indo-European "one-handed" god: ________________
6. The chief god of the Zoroastrian religion: ________________
7. The First Battle of Mag Tuired was fought between the Tuatha Dé Danann and the ________________.
8. The Roman historian Tacitus wrote the work entitled ________________.
9. A third-function representative among the Aməša Spəntas: ________________
10. While Caesar's "Mercury" probably corresponds to Irish Lug, his "Jupiter" should likely be identified with Irish ________________.
11. A collection of Irish tales concerned chiefly with the great king Conchobar and the warrior Cúchulainn: ________________
12. Norse god corresponding to Indic Varuṇa: ________________
13. "Second function" within the first function of Irish society: ________________
14. A triple-sinning warrior: ________________
15. The evil-eyed grandfather of Lug; he killed Nuada: ________________
16. The poet and judge among the Milesians: ________________

Answers: *Odin, Fomoire, St. Patrick, Partholón, Amairgin, Vohu Manah, Ogma, the Dagda, Ulster Cycle, Fir Bolg, Tyr, Śiśupala, Jarasaṁdha, Gallic War, Ahura Mazdah, Kurukṣetra, Zarathuštra, Life of the Caesars, Germania, Filid, Cessair, St. Nicholas, Lebor Gabála Érenn, Armaiti, Thor, Balor*

Exam 3–1, page 2

1. Paṇḍu's first wife: ____________________

2. The king who replaced Nuada and oppressed his mother's people:

   ____

3. A reformer of Iranian religion: ____________________

4. Duhṣanta and Śakuntala are married in the ____________________ style.

5. The goddess Hel rules over ____________________.

6. This goddess became human to give birth to Dyaus and other Vasus:

   ____

7. Many Indo-European religious terms are preserved only in Celtic, Italic, and ____________________.

8. In the thirteenth year of exile, this son of Paṇḍu disguised himself as a cook/butcher: ____________________

9. Horatius Cocles is the Roman reflex of the ____________________ god.

10. Etruscan leader whose help Tarquinius recruited in his bid to retake Rome: ____________________

11. The oldest of the sons of Dhṛtaraṣṭra: ____________________

12. Sister of Kṛṣṇa and Arjuna's second wife: ____________________

13. Trickster god who fathered Fenrir: ____________________

14. Satyavati's "other" son, he produces offspring by the widows of Vicitravirya: ____________________

15. A third-function deity in the Gallic pantheon as described by Julius Caesar: ____________________

16. The first of the Milesians to be killed by the Tuatha Dé Danann:

    ____

17. The letters of the early Germanic alphabets are called

    ____________________.

***Answers:** Nakula, Íth, Ganga, Bhima, Loki, Droṇa, Ogma, Donn, Gandhari, Bifröst, Indo-Iranian, Vohu Manah, one-legged, Brahmin, Gandharva, Nemed, logograms, Bricriu, Bres, Subhadra, runes, one-eared, Apollo, Duryodhana, Niflheim, Kunti, Zarathuštra, one-handed, Germanic, Vyasa, Sarasvati, one-eyed, Draupadi, Vidura, Lars Porsenna*

Exam 3–1, page 3

1. Indra sent this Apsara to seduce a powerful ascetic: ________________

2. The first invaders to come to Ireland were led by __________________.

3. According to Lucan, ____________________ is one of the gods to whom the Celts offer human sacrifice.

4. The name that Caesar gives to the third function of Gallic (Celtic) society: ___________________

5. This group of invaders divided Ireland into five provinces: ___________________

6. One of the biographical works written by Snorri Sturluson: ___________________

7. A metaphorical expression, such as "wave traveler" (meaning "boat") used in early Germanic literature: ___________________

8. The collection of Irish tales concerned with the Tuatha Dé Danann: ___________________

9. The Aməša Spənta that likely shares a common origin with Vedic Varuṇa: ___________________

10. A skillful gambler who defeated Yudhiṣṭhira and sent the Paṇḍavas into exile: ___________________

11. The third-function figures in the Second Battle of Mag Tuired: ___________________

12. Wise giant in Norse tradition who guards the well of wisdom: ___________________

13. The great "world-tree" in Norse tradition; Odin hanged himself from it: ___________________

14. A dragon slayer who is typical of Odin's chivalrous warriors: ___________________

15. One of the two most important poems of the *Poetic Edda:*

    ____

16. Frey's magical ship: ____________________

17. The sole survivor of the second wave of invaders to come to Ireland:

    ____

***Answers:** Mythological Cycle, berserkir, Yggdrasil, Skadi, Voluspá, History of the Danes, Math, Tuan, Midgard, Menaka, the Milesians, hyperbole, Esus, Sahadeva, Fir Bolg, Sreng, Ulster Cycle, Mada, kenning, Mimir, Cessair, Plebes, Fomoire, Sigurd, Equites, Jupiter, Partholón, Śakuni, Aša Vahišta, Egils Saga, Ogma, Skithblathnir*

Practice Exam 3–2

Choose the most correct answer from the list at the bottom of the page and write that answer in the space at the end of the question. A single answer can be used only once. Not every possible answer will be used.

1. The Indo-European divine "twins" of Scandinavia: ___________________
2. Iranian Armaiti is opposed by _____________________, strengthening her identification with Indic Sarasvati.
3. The first wave of invaders to settle Ireland were led by a granddaughter of ___________________.
4. Beginning with the persecution of Irish Druids, this group expanded their realm of influence: ___________________
5. Roman reflex of the Proto-Indo-European "one-handed" god: ___________________
6. A second-function representative among the Aməša Spəntas: ___________________
7. The Second Battle of Mag Tuired appears to be the Irish reflex of the Proto-Indo-European tradition about a war between ___________________
8. Tacitus tells us about this Germanic goddess who appears to correspond to the Norse god Njord: ___________________
9. This general of Magadha was decapitated by Kṛṣṇa: ___________________
10. While Caesar's "Mercury" probably corresponds to Irish Lug, his "Apollo" should likely be identified with: ___________________
11. A collection of stories concerned principally with Fionn mac Cumhaill: ___________________
12. He is the father of Fenrir and a trickster: ___________________

13. According to Caesar, what is the chief belief of the Druids?

____

14. One of the two great epics of ancient India: ____________________

15. After Droṇa's death, this one takes over as general of the Kaurava army: ____________________

16. The Avestan counterpart of Vedic Rudra; he was demonized:

____

Answers: *the Bards, Mucius Scaevola, Ramayaṇa, Ulster Cycle, Minerva, Nāṅhaithya, Arjuna, the eternal nature of the soul, Noah, the functions; Vili and Ve; Cocles, Loki; Njord and Frey; good and evil; Xšathra, Nerthus, Śiśupala, Filid, Dian Cécht, Karṇa, Thor, the Book of the Conquests of Ireland, the goodness of humanity, Saurva, Fenian Cycle, Yajur Veda, Indra*

Exam 3–2, page 2

1. The thief who stole Mjollnir: ___________________
2. A biographical work written by Snorri Sturluson: ___________________
3. The battle that marks the end of time in Viking tradition: ___________________
4. Following the reforms of Zarathuštra, this god expands his realm of influence, even becoming a warrior deity: ___________________
5. The god that Zarathuštra elevated to a position far above all other gods: ___________________
6. King of Magadha: ___________________
7. The Viking reflex of the Proto-Indo-European "one-eyed" god: ___________________
8. His followers were oppressed by the Fomoire and fled away in three groups of ten: ___________________
9. Tyr is affiliated with the Germanic legal assembly, the ___________________.
10. One of the "materials" from which the fetter was made that bound Fenrir: ___________________
11. The husband of Cessair who survived the flood and who had the ability to change himself into animals: ___________________
12. Norse goddess of fertility and sensuality: ___________________
13. Wise one who is killed while trying to negotiate an end to a war: ___________________
14. A Celtic cultural phase: ___________________
15. A day bearing the name of a Germanic deity: ___________________

16. From his blood, the dwarves created the mead that makes one a poet:

____

17. German composer whose operatic *Ring* cycle is based on the *Nibelungenlied:* _________________

Answers: *Jarasaṁdha, Kvasir, iron, Thrym, Loki, Yggdrasil, Poetic Edda, Lug, Monday, Moot, Leiden, Thing, Varuṇa, La Tène, St. Olaf's Saga, Well of Wisdom, Wagner, Odin, Ragnarök, Nemed, Mimir, Fintan, Mithra, bird spittle, Ahura Mazdah, Partholón, Mahler, Bergelmir, Indra, Math, Wednesday, Freya, Mada, Brynhild*

Exam 3–2, page 3

1. The Indo-European warrior-type that is represented by Arjuna in India is represented by ________________ in Greece.

2. He is a reflex of the Proto-Indo-European "cross-dressing warrior," but not of the triple-sinning warrior: ________________

3. One of the celebrated Norse *berserkir:* ________________

4. Druidism in Britain effectively came to an end with the ________________.

5. The Iranian language in which the Zoroastrian sacred book is written: ________________

6. In the Norse theogony, the world is created from the dismembered body of this cosmic giant: ________________

7. The name of the warrior class in ancient Iran: ________________

8. A Welsh sorcerer who is changed into three different animals (of two different genders): ________________

9. Urvaśi left this husband when she saw him illuminated by a lightning flash: ________________

10. The portion of the Avesta attributed to Zarathuštra himself: ________________

11. The name that Caesar gives to the second function of Gallic (Celtic) society: ________________

12. In the First Battle of Mag Tuired, the Tuatha Dé Danann fight against the ________________.

13. The earliest known Germanic literary work: ________________

14. According to Caesar, the Druids are exempt from ________________.

15. Bhiṣma's Nordic counterpart: ________________

16. He is admitted to the house of Nuada because he possesses all skills: ____________________

17. A Celtic language of Asia Minor: ____________________

Answers: *Bjarki, charcoal, Avestan, war tax, Achilles, Sigurd, Thor, human sacrifice, Galatian, Njord, Pururavas, Puruṣa, Heracles, Fomoire, the Poetic Edda, Lug, Gwydion, Sreng, Heimdall, Goibniu, rajanyas, Ymir, Pahlavi, Horatius, Gathas, the Gothic Bible, the Battle of Mona, Fir Bolg, Equites, Nar, Videvdat, Old Persian, the arrival of Christianity, Celtiberian*

Answers to Practice Exams

Practice Exam 1–1

Page 1

1. *Lithuanian*
2. *Ferdinand de Saussure*
3. *Russian Formalism*
4. *Romulus*
5. *the army*
6. *Janus*
7. *Pontifex Maximus*
8. *Phocis*
9. *Tarquinius Superbus*
10. *Acca Larentia*
11. *Circus Maximus*
12. *Armenian*
13. *Penates*
14. *the Pontic Steppe*

Page 2

1. *Ea*
2. *Numa Pompilius*
3. *Chaos*
4. *Apollodorus*
5. *Typhoeus*
6. *Astarte*
7. *arbor felix*
8. *Amulius*
9. *third*
10. *Horatius*
11. *Cronus*
12. *Rex Sacrorum*
13. *Metis*
14. *Quirinus*
15. *Sea Peoples*

Page 3

1. *Eurynome*
2. *Linear B*
3. *Stultorum feriae*
4. *Erinyes*
5. *Minoan*
6. *Enuma Elish*
7. *Titus Tatius*
8. *Aventine*
9. *Leto*
10. *Oedipus*
11. *Elysian Islands*
12. *Aeneas*
13. *Jupiter*
14. *Campus sceleratus*
15. *Selene*

Practice Exam 1–2

Page 1

1. *Hittite*
2. *Lévi-Strauss*
3. *functions*
4. *Rex Sacrorum*
5. *dog*
6. *funeral pyre*

7/8. *Mars, Quirinus*

9. *Tarquinius Priscus*
10. *Robigalia*
11. *Goidelic*
12. *Lares*
13. *Consus*
14. *Pons Sublicius*

Page 2

1/2. *legal, magical*

3. *Salii*
4. *Prometheus*
5. *Gaea*
6. *copper cutting tool*
7. *Cronus*
8. *Linear B*
9. *Romulus*
10. *Cyclopes*
11. *Metis*
12. *Numa*
13. *horse*
14. *Saussure*
15. *Ascanius*

Page 3

1. *Tesub*
2. *Hyperion*
3. *Aphrodite*
4. *Faustulus*
5. *Norse*
6. *Sabines*
7. *Sea Peoples*
8. *cognates*
9. *Janus*
10. *grain*
11. *Amalthea*
12. *Equus October*
13. *Ops*
14. *Quirinus*
15. *Romulus*

Practice Exam 2–1

Page 1

1. *Dryad*
2. *Clotho*
3. *Omphale*
4. *Naiad*
5. *Semele*
6. *Deianira*
7. *Persephone*
8. *Europa*
9. *Smintheus*
10. *Alcmena*
11. *Athena*
12. *shield of Achilles*
13. *Cerberus*
14. *Lernaean Hydra*
15. *Subura*
16. *king*

Page 2

1. *Apollo*
2. *Mitra*
3. *Maryanni*
4. *Indra*
5. *Puṣan*
6. *Lycurgus*
7. *Centaurus*
8. *childbirth*
9. *Tullus Hostilius*
10. *Perkunas*
11. *Augeas*
12. *satyr*
13. *Atalanta*
14. *Śiva*
15. *Iole*
16. *Śri*
17. *white*

Page 3

1. *mariners*
2. *Agni*
3. *Apsaras*
4. *Hippolyta*
5. *Vasus*
6. *Rhadamanthys*
7. *Triśiras*
8. *Horatius*
9. *Proteus*
10. *Bhaga*
11. *Tyndareus*
12. *Hephaestus*
13. *Maruts*
14. *bull*
15. *Asclepius*
16. *Gautama*
17. *Fjörgyn(n)*

Practice Exam 2–2

Page 1

1. *Artemis*
2. *Odysseus*
3. *Omphale*
4. *Oreads*
5. *Dionysus*
6. *Heracles*
7. *Nessus*
8. *Pentheus*
9. *Callisto*
10. *Iphicles*
11. *Orthus*
12. *Geryon*
13. *the Fates*
14. *Lernaean Hydra*
15. *Lucretia*
16. *Atharva*

Page 2

1. *Hermaphroditus*
2. *Maruts*
3. *Melampus*
4. *Arachne*
5. *Hebe*
6. *Namuci*
7. *Mettius Fuffetius*
8. *Agamemnon*
9. *clone*
10. *Ino*
11. *Varuṇa*
12. *Vasus*
13. *Mitanni*
14. *Stymphalian*
15. *Viṣṇu*
16. *chariot race*
17. *gandharvas*

Page 3

1. *thyrsus*
2. *sky god*
3. *Iphicles*
4. *Manu*
5. *Hephaestus*
6. *Marsyas*
7. *horses*
8. *Dioscuri*
9. *Vṛtra*
10. *constellations*
11. *Rudra*
12. *Ares*
13. *Indra*
14. *Atlas*
15. *Sarasvati*
16. *Iphigenia*
17. *Apam Napat*

Practice Exam 3–1

Page 1

1. *Ogma*
2. *St. Patrick*
3. *Partholón*
4. *Kurukṣetra*
5. *Tyr*
6. *Ahura Mazdah*
7. *Fir Bolg*
8. *Germania*
9. *Armaiti*
10. *The Dagda*
11. *Ulster Cycle*
12. *Odin*
13. *Filid*
14. *Śiśupala*
15. *Balor*
16. *Amairgin*

Page 2

1. *Kunti*
2. *Bres*
3. *Zarathuštra*
4. *Gandharva*
5. *Niflheim*
6. *Ganga*
7. *Indo-Iranian*
8. *Bhima*
9. *one-eyed*
10. *Lars Porsenna*
11. *Duryodhana*
12. *Subhadra*
13. *Loki*
14. *Vyasa*
15. *Apollo*
16. *Íth*
17. *runes*

Page 3

1. *Menaka*
2. *Cessair*
3. *Esus*
4. *Plebes*
5. *Fir Bolg*
6. *Egils Saga*
7. *kenning*
8. *Mythological Cycle*
9. *Aša Vahišta*
10. *Śakuni*
11. *Fomoire*
12. *Mimir*
13. *Yggdrasil*
14. *Sigurd*
15. *Voluspá*
16. *Skithblathnir*
17. *Tuan*

Practice Exam 3–2

Page 1

1. *Njord and Frey*
2. *Nañhaithya*
3. *Noah*
4. *Filid*
5. *Mucius Scaevola*
6. *Xšathra*
7. *the functions*
8. *Nerthus*
9. *Śiśupala*
10. *Dian Cécht*
11. *Fenian Cycle*
12. *Loki*
13. *the eternal nature of the soul*
14. *Ramayaṇa*
15. *Karṇa*
16. *Saurva*

Page 2

1. *Thrym*
2. *St. Olaf's Saga*
3. *Ragnarök*
4. *Mithra*
5. *Ahura Mazdah*
6. *Jarasaṁdha*
7. *Odin*
8. *Nemed*
9. *Thing*
10. *bird spittle*
11. *Fintan*
12. *Freya*
13. *Mimir*
14. *La Tène*
15. *Wednesday*
16. *Kvasir*
17. *Wagner*

Page 3

1. *Achilles*
2. *Thor*
3. *Bjarki*
4. *Battle of Mona*
5. *Avestan*
6. *Ymir*
7. *Nar*
8. *Gwydion*
9. *Pururavas*
10. *Gathas*
11. *Equites*
12. *Fir Bolg*
13. *the Gothic Bible*
14. *war tax*
15. *Heimdall*
16. *Lug*
17. *Galatian*